The Social Agent

The Social Agent

A TRUE INTRIGUE OF
SEX, SPIES, AND HEARTBREAK
BEHIND THE IRON CURTAIN

Charles Laurence

IVAN R. DEE   CHICAGO   2010

www.ivanrdee.com

Library of Congress Cataloging-in-Publication Data:
Laurence, Charles, 1950–
The social agent : a true intrigue of sex, spies, and heartbreak behind the
Iron Curtain / Charles Laurence.
p. cm.
Includes index.
ISBN 978-1-56663-845-6 (cloth : alk. paper)
1. Laurence, Charles, 1950– —Childhood and youth. 2. British—Czech
Republic—Prague—Biography. 3. Prague (Czech Republic)—Biography.
4. Prague (Czech Republic)—Social life and customs—20th century.
5. Diplomats—Family relationships—Czech Republic—Prague—History—20th
century. 6. Espionage, British—Czech Republic—Prague—History—20th
century. 7. Communism—Europe, Eastern—History—20th century. I. Title.
DB2629.L38A3 2010
327.124104371'2092—dc22
[B]   2009029396

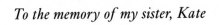

To the memory of my sister, Kate

Acknowledgments

This story could not have been told without the skill and efforts in Prague of Jan Stojaspal. My thanks go to Tom Lansner for his support, Rob McQuilkin for believing in me, my parents Sir Peter and Lady Laurence for their interesting lives, and, especially, with affection, to Carole Smith for her unfailing faith and enthusiasm.

C. L.

Woodstock, New York
November 2009

The Social Agent

One

Prague when I knew it as a boy was a city of fear and spies and sooty fogs. It was behind the Iron Curtain, that much I understood at seven. We would drive through its barriers of concrete block houses, barbed wire, and no-man's-land in the big grey Morris with a six-cylinder engine and red leather seats, bought because my father deemed it tough enough for duty on the other side. That other side was spooky—spooky in the exciting way of stories we read in adventure magazines.

It's strange the things you remember. The roads were rougher, and there was danger of some kind because we were going into enemy territory. I knew about enemies as this was 1957, and you could not be growing up in England in 1957 without knowing about enemies. There had been the War. In London it had left gaps in the buildings with half-hidden rubble behind rusting corrugated fences, empty holes that Granny blamed on people called Bosch, Krauts, and Bloody Germans. They had tried to kill Granny with bombs, and while they hadn't killed her they had killed a lot of other people. They wore jackboots. We knew what they looked like from the illustrations in those magazines and comic books.

The soldiers at the red-and-white barrier that blocked the road to Prague wore similar jackboots. They had guns and, I think, grey uniforms. They may have been khaki green. There were woods in the background. Dad would stop the car and roll down the window. He would tell us kids to be quiet while he handed over a bundle of passports and let the soldiers know that he was a diplomat, on his way to the British embassy in Prague. Vienna was to the south, behind us, another city of spies. Vienna and Prague both; one city on our side, one on the other.

Of course, this enemy was different. These weren't Germans; they were Russians and Czechs, who only a decade before had been our friends, according to the chat at the family supper table. Now they guarded the Iron Curtain. This was the Cold War.

Father said we had permission to go to Czechoslovakia. Even with official permission, though, it was a long wait for the soldiers to bring back the passports. Whenever we came and went, the barrier would be down across the road and we would have to wait, but eventually it would go up and we could drive on, slowly. We could not actually see an Iron Curtain, only barbed wire strung between watchtowers, and sometimes dogs—big Alsatians with dark muzzles and low lopes, held back on straining leashes.

I have no memory of arriving in Prague, only of the first night we spent there. We booked into a grand hotel, or at least an old-fashioned one that seemed grand at the time. We didn't have to carry our own suitcases. I shared a room with my sister,

Kate, while Nanny with my baby brother had another, and my parents a third, all along a long white corridor with a carpet that muffled our footsteps so we could get away with running indoors. That was a good thing, because it was a frigid November, and outside on the streets there was nothing but dirty, gritty snow. The room had only one bed, a double, which, though Kate and I had always shared a room, was a change for us. There was a heavy down quilt too, instead of blankets. We ate stew with dumplings in a big empty dining room. I loved those dumplings and asked for more. Later Mother, or perhaps it was Father, sat on the end of the bed and made shadow animals on the wall with their hands.

We all stayed in that hotel for quite a while, because apparently it was hard to find a house. But then Kate and I were used to the idea of moving from one home to another: that was all we had known. Kate was eight, and I was seven. We had already lived in Athens, which I couldn't remember, Trieste in Italy, and London. Now we would be here in Prague. We learned to say "dobrý den," which means "good day."

One afternoon a tall man staying in the hotel took me to an ice hockey match. He knew about ice hockey because he was Canadian, and in Canada they played ice hockey just as they did in Prague, even though Canada was somehow English. The players skated amazingly fast on the ice rink and seemed to crash into one another intentionally, which was fun, though I never actually went to another ice hockey match.

While we ate our stew with dumplings, which seemed to be supper every day, my parents would talk about how we had to wait to have our own home, because over here you couldn't just go out and find one. Instead you had to have permission from the men in charge, the government, just as we had received permission to come here in the first place. The men who ran the government were Communists. This was the problem. They wanted to tell us where to live while my parents argued that they themselves should have a choice in the matter. Mother wanted a house with a garden, which seemed to be particularly difficult to find; and Dad said that the government officials were making us take a place where another family could live downstairs and "watch" us. Why? It was another thing that had to do with them being on the enemy side, and apparently they wanted to know everything we were doing.

Eventually we drove to a suburb called Barrandov, at the top of a wooded hill, and continued along a road covered in icy snow. At first, as the car began to slide, we were nervous. After a few moments, however, we got used to the sliding feeling, and the only time I remember being scared was when the car spun the whole way around, like a carnival ride. Mother said Barrandov was where the Czechs had a film studio and made movies, or at least had done so before the Communists came. I had not yet seen a movie, but Mother seemed pleased by the suggestion of glamour that the studio somehow lent the neighborhood—at least until we pulled up to the address that was meant for us.

"It is an incredibly ugly house," said Mother.

"There's a tape recorder with a microphone under the floor, so they can hear us talk," said Father. "The man downstairs is going to stoke the furnace and change the tapes. So we'll have to talk quietly—won't we?—so that he can't hear."

The house was dark grey, square, with square windows, which were double so we could grow plants between the inside window and the outside window, and it had a square balcony sticking out of the front. It had a flat roof too, which I don't think I had ever seen before. Now I would know to call it "functionalist." When we went to look in the garden, we found some brown rabbits in a hutch—they didn't seem to be cold—and a small dirty swimming pool covered in greenish ice. I tried to smash the ice with a stick, but couldn't.

In front of the house was a steep downhill drive leading to a garage. Dad said it would be hard to get up and down it in this snow, but that he was going to fit chains on the wheels of the car so they could grip the pavement properly. When he did, they made a lot of noise. Soon some men came carrying crates into the house, familiar crates, and that was exciting, because inside them would be all our stuff. When he found his toolbox, Dad took out a hammer and a pair of pliers and made a sled out of one of the packing crates. What I remember best is how he nailed a metal band that had been strapped around the crates to the edges of the wood that ran on the snow, which he said would make the sled go faster. Kate and I then took turns rocketing down the icy drive.

It was the kind of thing he'd always done. Just the year before, on our summer holiday, my father had made bows and arrows out of tree branches and sticks. But after that sled, after Prague, he didn't seem to make things any more. He wasn't the same.

By the time we moved to Barrandov, Kate and I were back at school. It was my second school, a French lycée, and I hated it. My parents explained that it was the only school in the whole of Prague that we could go to, because all the others were Communist and intended for Czechs. Mother got us stiff leather satchels with two straps that went over our shoulders, as with a knapsack. All the kids had them, but even then they seemed old-fashioned, like the green ink and quills we would use for writing. We had to speak French, and the teacher was named Monsieur Gareau. I didn't like him, and he didn't like me. I was never a good schoolboy, frankly, at least not at lessons. But Kate did very well at school, and Monsieur Gareau was quite friendly with her. I do not remember learning French, but I did speak it—I had to—and even now it bursts onto my tongue when I am in France and find myself either drunk or angry.

Dad drove us to school on his way to the embassy. It was still dark when we set out in the mornings, and there was still snow in those first months, the tire chains making even more noise on the old cobbled roads at the city center. We would drive down long streets with tall, dirty buildings that seemed to go on for block after block, without any spaces in between. Some had statues over grand doorways and elaborate carvings under their roofs, but most were flat and covered in what looked like grey concrete—everything square, just as at our house. In the windows were yellow lights, when there were any lights at all, while the ground-floor windows giving onto the sidewalk were usually covered by thick, dungeonlike bars, unless they were shop windows. These were no bigger than the other windows, and you could hardly see inside for all the sausages hanging from racks and loaves of bread and cabbages and cans stacked behind the glass in great piles. Others had shoes or clothes in them, but they certainly looked nothing like the shops and department stores Mother had taken us to in London and Trieste. Prague was different.

When you got out of the car there was a strange, acrid smell which got right up into your nasal passages, where it burned slightly. Dad said it was the bad petrol the Czechs used. It even made the fog look yellow, though that was also because of the coal people burned in their stoves and fireplaces, more brown than black on this side of the Iron Curtain. To this day I can feel that smell in my nose.

There was a strange driving rule then which has gone now, and it was called "the rule of the right." At least that is how Dad explained it while we were driving to school one day. It meant that when you wanted to turn left at an intersection, you first pulled into the street coming in from the right before turning hard to the left and waiting for the traffic lights to change. That way, you never turned left across the oncoming traffic or the trams, which had right-of-way on the rails that ran down the center of the streets.

We would wait for the lights to change, the wipers going swoosh-swoosh, watching the cars go by. Quite a few of them were Tatras, the biggest of the Communist cars, and they were a riveting sight. They looked like no other car I had ever seen, and, having been living abroad with my family, I had seen more than most. Tatras looked like sharks on wheels, long black sharks. They often had black windows too. The shape was humpbacked and completely smooth, with the headlights set behind glass panels that ran the whole way across the front. There were no visible wheel arches as the tires disappeared completely beneath the vehicle's great streamlined bulk, and the back, where the engine was, sloped away like a stretched-out Volkswagen Beetle. But the thing that really set this car apart was this: running down that sloping back, set between twin rear windows, was a great big shark's fin.

"They're all secret police cars," Dad explained. "Ordinary people never get them."

Mother said: "Can you just imagine the sort of things that happen in them? The sort of things they do in those cars?"

I tried. I thought of secret policemen strangling someone behind the smoked glass, strangling someone with a rope wrapped around his neck.

It's all changed, of course. The streets may be the same streets, and most of the same buildings still stand, but they look very different, if only because today the grime of war and poverty and communism has been almost entirely washed away. The past—even the very distant past of a medieval city that escaped both nineteenth-century money and twentieth-century bombs—has been restored or painted over to within an inch of its life since 1989 when the Velvet Revolution put an end to the Communist dictatorship. Dad always said that the dark times did not suit the Czechs, who were a creative people with a strong, sardonic sense of humor. So to some extent the fresh paint and the restoration of democratic government have given them back their city. But returning to Prague some fifty years later—a gap of time hard enough to accept in itself—the place, to me, looks fake. Like one of those black-and-white movies tinted up for modern audiences. And so it takes a while to align today's Prague with the postcards I long ago stuck in albums and stashed away in my old school trunk.

The trams are in much brighter orange now, but not a Tatra anywhere. The girl at the hotel reception desk says that she knows the car I mean when I describe the shark's fin, but the only one she can think of is in the Technical Museum, which turns out to be closed for renovation. Which makes sense: both that the technical achievements of the Communist world, generally second-rate, should be in a museum, and also that the museum itself, which appears to have been built in the same era, should need significant renovation.

I have turned down the hill of Seifertova Street to follow the trams toward the Vltava River, through the medieval town that has become such a roaring tourist attraction. First there are railway lines and a path threading loudly though a highway interchange, walls scrawled with graffiti that doesn't quite rise to the sense of urban threat I am used to in New York. In fact the graffiti in Prague—and there is a lot of it—still looks like a cry for freedom from history. People nod as we step out of each other's way, though they walk purposefully, as if attending to business. No longer do they scurry down the sidewalks, hugging the walls, eyes turned away as if bent on getting safely back indoors. Nor is there the sort of fog I remember, though it is February. The Gothic spires of the Týn Church in the Old Town Square pass in and out of view as I make my way around the narrow streets, silhouetted against a cold blue sky. There are cafés and bars and restaurants turning out the lunch crowd, and antique shops, mostly filled with junk and old porcelain teacups, which for some reason have always been considered treasure here in Eastern Europe, and even more souvenir shops, selling Bohemian garnets and the puppets that Czechs are known for. Indeed, the souvenir shops have taken over whole blocks in the narrowest, oldest streets, where I remember grocers and cheese shops selling yogurt in bottles with layers of jam at the bottom. There is a touch of Disney to the Old Town Square, and a lot of cheap beer. No wonder the tourists come, even in winter. All along the old coronation route are crowds without break. Finally, reaching the Charles Bridge, I can breathe again. The oldest functioning span in Europe, this bridge is uniquely decorated along its cobbled walkway with thirty-two statues of gods, martyrs, and heroes majestically spaced across its entire length, from the battle-scarred tower guarding one end to its mate at the other. The bridge, at least, is still mine. Footsteps on the cobbles still ring in my memory from crossings back and forth with Nanny and my brother in his pram, heading for the puppet theatres and the roast-chestnut stalls.

On the far side, above the north bank, Prague Castle rises above more ranks of medieval roofs and the wedding-cake domes of the newer Baroque. Once the seat of the Holy Roman Empire, the Pražský Hrad is also where, just twenty years ago, a stooped, cigarette-sucking playwright named Václav Havel strolled in to take his country back from the Communists. Only the Czechs could have a Velvet Revolution. They still say "To the Hrad!" when they aim to take over the government, and they mean it literally.

It is where I too am bound, climbing with aching knees the steep stepped street of Zámecké Schody to find the home of an old widow living at the back of Castle Square. I was there only once or twice, as a boy, but can still picture its medieval door with iron studs, set low against the flagstones of the sidewalk, opening to a Gothic vault with church statues and carvings and old chests, and then a staircase, a big wooden staircase leading up into a fantasy world, a palace room from a fairy tale, glittering, lined with books and enormous paintings and strange bedazzling objects. Perhaps it will be nothing like that when I see it as an adult, but the widow still lives there. I have found her telephone number and called her, and one thing I know for certain: this place is at the heart of the story I need to hear.

A rather ordinary-looking buzzer is located where maybe there should be a bell pull, and I press the button with an ear to the heavy wood. Then I step back a pace or two, as I know from being a newspaper reporter that often, when you are ringing the doorbells of strangers, people feel better if they can have a look at you before actually letting you in. On the other hand, while I remember Geraldine Mucha, or at least an impression of her, and have seen her caught in snapshots still glued into albums on the bottom shelves of the bookcase in my parents' house, she is not likely to recognize me now.

In my mind Geraldine is a beautiful woman, an archetype of beauty almost, for that is how I've always heard her talked about. She came from Scotland, originally, and during the war had married a Czech named Jiří Mucha, though we always called him George. Today Prague is plastered with the name of Mucha, plastered on every billboard and poster wall, it seems, not to mention outside the Mucha museum and the Mucha brasserie and any number of Mucha shops. All of which celebrate and profit from the life and work of Alphonse Mucha, Jiří's father and a famous Art Nouveau artist who made a fortune in the Belle Epoch of Paris at the turn of the twentieth century. Even today his name is synonymous with the sensuous, twirling posters he painted, advertising things like cigarette rolling papers and bicycles, all featuring lovely girls with flowing hair and breasts exposed. Most famously of all, he created posters for Sarah Bernhardt, whose theatrical performances provided the most fashionable nights out in Paris. Eventually French Art Nouveau—in everything from jewelry and teacups and wine jugs to paintings and figurines—became known simply as "Le Style Mucha," and its rather saccharine magic will be immediately familiar to anyone growing up in the 1960s. Mucha's posters for Job cigarette papers, in particular, with wreaths of smoke, were huge hits in hippie head shops while art books with yet *more* lovely breasts and rounded hips decorated the coffee tables of zeitgeist-friendly couples. I was always proud to know where they had come from. But I am stunned to find Mucha at the heart of Prague's tourist boom. I had no idea. There is Mucha everywhere.

In one of our old photographs, Geraldine is in a bathing suit on a lakeside beach, reclining at a picnic. I assume my parents were the hosts. She has her right knee up, clutched in both hands, and her head is back, hair tumbling. She has turned toward the camera and is laughing, her mouth open and dimples falling from high cheekbones. "Geraldine's always doing that laugh," I remember Mother saying once. "It's a nervous laugh of course, just a nervous laugh." Mother always was the mistress of the put-down. None better. Another time, tempering her barb with just a bit more sympathy, she said: "She had a rotten time when George was in jail. John was just a baby, and they had nothing. She lived on potatoes for three years. And charity." I wondered about living on potatoes for three whole years, and charity.

I hear a window open on the second floor, above the door and a foot or so to the left. It seems to be a kind of watchman's hatch, just a pane or two of a much larger window. "Oh, there you are!" says Geraldine, poking her entire head through the window for a better view. "I'll come right down." The first thing I notice about her is that her clean British tones have been unchanged by so many years of guttural Czech. It takes a minute or two for her to get down, for this is a big old house, and Geraldine is just short of her ninetieth birthday. But then I hear the churning of ancient locks.

"Come in, come in," she says, and laughs. Of course she laughs. She must be wondering why I'm here. I hand her flowers, and she smiles, I think with real pleasure, because even today flowers in winter are rather harder to come by here than in London or New York. She takes a sniff, ushers me forward, and carefully secures the door behind me. Her face is beaten by age but still beautiful, a beautiful old woman's face. I am relieved by that. The cheekbones are unbowed, the eyes wide spaced and greyish blue—the left one watery and irritated, so she wipes it—the golden hair now white with a little grey, but the chin line still defined. A classic face, with grace, proportioned just so. She is wearing a big black sweater dashingly embroidered with red flowers and tasseled gold chains, over a simple black dress, refusing to quite concede to ninety. I wonder if she has dressed up for tea. I wonder if she has served as a template for all my wives.

Two

H ow are your parents?" asks Geraldine as we sit down. She has climbed the stairs spryly enough and boasted, "Oh, I'm a tough old stick!" She has waved a hand vaguely through the grand gallery of the living room, perhaps a hundred feet by fifty, lined at the east end with library shelves of leather-bound books and cracked-spine paperbacks, and at the west with side tables and knickknacks and frame-to-frame artworks. Chairs and settees lie old and empty in random groups, as if waiting for the party to start up again. There are stuffed birds in glass cases, tapestries, huge gilt mirrors, chandeliers, and heavy drapes. "You see, all the old treasures are still here." A life-size Mucha poster of Bernhardt as Medea—a bloodstained knife in hand and lifeless children at her feet—hangs on the south wall by a window.

"Father's fine," I answer. "He's showing his age at last, but he is still the man completely in control. As for Mother, well, you know. She'll go on complaining of her headaches until she's a hundred and ten."

I look closely at Geraldine at this first mention of Mother. She dabs at the weeping eye with a handkerchief. "So sorry. It's nothing, some little infection. Clearing up. . . . Your mother. Yes. How old is she? I always forget. And it has been years!"

"Eighty," I reply. "Dad's eighty-four. Both have just had their birthdays."

"Eighty? Of course! She was ten years younger than I," says Geraldine, slowly, an emphasis on "was." Certainly Mother was never any fewer than ten years younger. But Geraldine is thinking of the time when Mother lifted her skirts for Jiří, fell in love as she so loved to do, and ran around Prague giddy at her conquest. For Jiří was a most attractive man. And this was the husband Geraldine had waited for through prison. So it had hurt that Mother, at thirty-three, was ten years younger, with firmer flesh, no doubt, than Geraldine, and not yet worn. I had not thought of that.

But Geraldine is calm. Her interest seems only passing. We have taken refuge, in this room, from ancient chill. It faces southeast, overlooking the bare trees of the Castle Square to the gates of the Hrad. Beyond them the black spire of the cathedral stands against the sky like a gun sight. Everything Geraldine now needs has contracted into the confines of her room. Her four poster bed, with curtains against the draft, is set just behind a baby grand piano, covered in sheet music, where she still drills and transcribes. For Geraldine is a concert pianist and a composer, and she keeps busy. She has a desk piled with diaries and writing paper and an old-fashioned telephone. In one corner is a dresser in wood so dark it seems jet black in the dimming light, the worn figures carved at its base barely visible. The bottom half, Geraldine tells me, is very old and had been an altar, salvaged from a monastery. Above the fireplace, where she cooks her suppers on a single gas ring to save a journey all the way to the kitchen, a horned devil is carved rampant into the black marble mantel. Precisely what he is up to is not quite clear, but he has a wicked look.

The Roman Catholic church still owns this old house, a palace going back five hundred years. "Oh yes," says Geraldine. "This is not the house that Alphonse built when he came home from Paris with his fortune and treasures. That was a villa, one of those terribly grand houses on the top of the hill. We lived there in Alphonse's old studio on the top floor when Jiří brought me home after the war. But then it was taken by the Communists. Some men came around one morning with a big truck—it must have been in 1949—and told us to get out. Just get out. They were from the Party, and the Party was taking the house so the Chinese could have it. They started packing up the furniture.

"Jiří would have none of it. He had no fear, you know. No fear at all. He shouted at them and told them they were so ignorant they had no idea that this was culture, that the house was a national treasure. 'Who's the idiot who gave the order to do this?' he shouted so loudly they must have heard him clear across Prague! But Jiří did the right thing, because the man in charge suddenly had doubts and went away to check with his bosses that he should be doing this.

"Then Jiří got on the telephone to someone he knew in the Party and to the mayor of Prague, because he always knew everyone. The men who came for you would cut your phone line so you couldn't call for help. But although they had cut the phone to the main house where my mother-in-law lived, they hadn't cut the phone we had upstairs, so Jiří used that.

"The man in the Party said they needed the house, but he gave us three weeks to go, so at least Jiří could get everything out and save it. He also persuaded the Catholics to rent us this house. So that's how we got here. And the Communists were never able to take it from the church."

The family has the old villa back now, but it came too late for Jiří, who died in 1991. He had always smoked too much, and Mother would say that the coal mines he had been forced to work in had broken his health. Jiří did well if that was true. He lived to seventy-six and saw the Velvet Revolution. He even saw some of the books he had written come back in print. But it had been John, Jiří's son, who had got the villa's property title back.

Geraldine is laughing again, softly. She has become skinny with age, her chest gone flat. Now she is maneuvering carefully around the coffee table set before the fire, brushing against the devil in the mantel, pouring water from the kettle into a china teapot. She has spooned out loose black tea and has a strainer ready in a saucer. There is Scottish shortbread in a tartan biscuit tin, a gift of nostalgia brought around by American diplomats showing the Mucha house to visitors. They still do that. "I'm a sort of museum nowadays. Do have some. Eat up!" There is a grace about her, an eagerness to please that must have been alluring once. In that old snapshot she is pleasing the camera like a movie star.

"Mother told me that you lived on potatoes when Jiří was in prison," I say.

"Oh, it wasn't quite as bad as that!"

Jiří Mucha had brazened it out with Communist bureaucrats from 1948, when old Uncle Joe Stalin seized Czechoslovakia for his Soviet empire, until 1951, when he was finally arrested. I was always told that he'd got away with it for as long as he did on the strength of the Mucha name. Back from wartime exile, Jiří lived in his palace full of treasures and was called the King of the Castle. But eventually the Communists arrested him, because Communists were all about hating aristocrats and Posh People, which would have included us. As kids hearing about all of this some ten years later, we could imagine the jackboots marching across the Castle Square when they came to get Jiří, or perhaps it was those men who wore black leather coats and drove Tatras.

There was the sense of a terrible injustice but also of something heroic. Jiří was the man who would sit at the head of the table, his head already balding above sweeping hair much longer than mine or Dad's, always holding a cigarette with smoke wafting over his face, his shoulders stooped by his suffering, his shirt open, telling stories in his soft, foreign voice, everyone's eyes fixed on him, rapt. Even then I think I understood that I had never met anyone quite like Jiří Mucha. Dad had been an officer in the War, had even won a major medal, but he never talked of *how*, and it was years before I ever learned the story. But Jiří was different. It was as if he were fighting the Commies single-handedly, and as if he were still fighting this war. Everyone wanted to be with him.

I had been just one year old in 1951 when he was taken away, and his own son John was three. This was only six years after Prague had been freed from the Germans, and before the Communists took over entirely. It is a timeline that says a lot about how Kate and I would later have seen things as we sat there and ate in the Mucha house.

"Food was short, that's true," says Geraldine. "We had no money. But I spent a lot of the time with my mother-in-law in Alphonse's house in Železná Ruda, an artists' colony in the country, much safer. And my mother-in-law managed to get country food, like eggs and vegetables." She does not use a name, just "mother-in-law." Alphonse, the old artist, had died in 1939 after the Nazis invaded—the day after they had taken him in for interrogation—and Geraldine had never known him.

"I really could have been reduced to feeding chickens and starving. After all, I was the wife of a convicted spy. But I was very lucky, because I was allowed to join the Musicians Union, and in those days of course you had to be in the union to work. That was how they controlled you. I worked in the publishing department because my father, you see, had always encouraged me with my music, and I had had a proper classical training, so I could read and write music. They needed people who could write music, and I transcribed scores for them. They would send them up to me in Železná, and I would send them back."

Geraldine says all this without bitterness, perhaps because it was so long ago. The hardships seem to have become quite natural to her; she was "lucky." And in a way she was. Others certainly suffered more. But until now I had had no idea that Jiří had been jailed as a spy. "Well," she says, "he wasn't *really* a spy." That charge was just an excuse to pick him up. They needed the excuse because they liked the cover of legitimacy, even with Stalin still alive and his KGB running things in the Czech State Security Police, the StB.

It would have been easy enough for them to frame Jiří, because there was not much of a line between keeping up friendships with foreigners and breaking Communist laws about giving them information. And Jiří liked to keep up friendships. Foreigners could still come and go back then, it seems, in the last years of the postwar 1940s as the Communists consolidated their power. He had grown up, after all, in Paris, New York, and Cape Cod, and, indeed, still had many friends in the West—writers, artists, and musicians. I always knew that, actually. Mother, who perhaps told a great many stories she didn't really mean the kids to hear, said that Jiří had had the run of his father's studio as a teenager, and that it was always filled with models with no clothes on, who spoiled him. That amused her. I later found out that his friends included famous people like the American novelist Philip Roth, who wrote a book about visiting Prague called *The Prague Orgy*; Peter Ustinov, the Russian émigré who became a Hollywood movie star; even Andy Warhol. His house was always full of people.

"It was his lifestyle," says Geraldine. She has a fond look on her face as she remembers this, but it is a little pained too. "This was the lifestyle he fought to keep up, manipulating the Party men, which he could do because he was very clever and, as I said, had no fear. Even after prison. He thought the Party men were stupid. Besides, he was a patriot. He didn't want to leave and be a beggar in someone else's country. That's what he would say, that if he ran away abroad he would be a beggar." When the dark days of Stalinist purges came, there were fewer visitors. "But we did have musicians who would be allowed in for concerts, and delegations of writers. And the diplomats: they liked to see Jiří. That's how we got to know your parents."

There were many women, not just Mother. They were actresses, models, artists, musicians. Philip Roth writes of teenage girls coming to stay from the Bohemian countryside, eager to try their luck on a life in the city; and they were fresh fruit for Jiří and his friends. I found obituaries in British newspapers which remembered him as "the Playboy of the Eastern World."

"Why didn't you just leave?" I ask Geraldine. Settled in an old wing chair hard up against the warmth of the fire, she looks shocked. "Because he was my husband. And he paid the price, the price in full."

Jiří had escaped the German invasion and joined the Czech Brigade in France, ready to fight. When the French collapsed, he dumped that uniform, got to Britain, and joined the Royal Air Force. Then he was attached to the Czech government in exile as a liaison officer and parlayed that into a role as a correspondent broadcasting to the European underground for the BBC. In that role he went around the world, following the battles in North Africa and the Middle East, and on the Western Front. He met Geraldine in London and married her in 1941. In London he worked on the side for the magazine *New Writing,* and on his novels. Dylan Thomas, Graham Greene, and Stephen Spender were among his friends. No wonder Mother was impressed.

"There was another reason I stayed in Prague," says Geraldine. "I couldn't *leave.* I didn't have a passport. I had come with Jiří in late 1945 as his wife, on his Czech passport. Maybe I shouldn't tell you this, but it was your father who managed to get me a passport, when he was at the embassy. He was in charge of passports because they didn't have a consul, who normally does them. It was quite a conspiracy!" Geraldine still has an alluring giggle. She leans forward, conspiratorially.

"It involved smuggling it in from Switzerland. He managed to get a passport-sized photo of me done here, and took it out with him to Switzerland, and got the passport made up and stamped. Then he gave it to me at one of Jiří's parties. It was terribly useful later. He was such a help."

There had been rumors that Jiří might have been a spy all along for the StB and its big brother, the KGB. These started in the 1960s, after our time in Prague, when he was allowed through the Iron Curtain to sell his father's pictures and the copyrights to all those posters that did so well. One obituary said these charges of espionage "greatly appealed to him." You could just hear his sardonic laugh. That same obituary said that he and Geraldine had had a son and a daughter. "Oh, no, they did not," said Mother when I spoke to her on the telephone after she had sent me a copy back in 1991. "It must be embarrassing for Geraldine. The daughter wasn't hers: she came from George's mistress."

When we were kids I always thought John seemed tentative around his dad. Tall for his age, he wore glasses, had bony knees, and did not like roughhouse games. "Actually, Jiří couldn't abide John," Geraldine says. "He never had Jiří's sense of adventure, his fearlessness. He certainly wasn't interested in art, and he never wanted to take a risk. Jiří would call him 'the bureaucrat.'"

Picking my moment, I tell Geraldine that I have seen a report from Radio Prague saying that a secret-police file on Jiří had been found, and that it was the file of a "collaborator."

"Nonsense!" says Geraldine. "Jiří never spied! Anyway, John got his own copy of that file. All it means is that when Jiří got out of the camp, he agreed to cooperate with the police because he *had* to, in order to get out. They all had to do it. It was the only way to survive. It was the only way Jiří could keep his home, his lifestyle. But of course he never told them anything but nonsense. They got so fed up with him that they fired him after a few years. That's in the file too."

"But they let him cross the Iron Curtain."

"Yes. Jiří did do a deal with the Party on that," says Geraldine. She rubs her fingers together in a universal gesture. "They wanted the money. The hard currency. They took half and let us keep the rest."

I am not sure whether to believe her. But in any case Geraldine has had enough. She is tired and is going out soon for a concert, a recital by a local quartet. Friends will be picking her up. "Careful not to get cold," I say. "It is getting cold outside."

"Oh, I meant to ask," she says suddenly. "How's Kate? *She* was really John's friend, I think, because she was older than you, and he was older too. They were such good friends. What became of her?"

"Kate's dead," I say. I don't even know where to begin, adding simply: "She got sick in Prague, at the end."

"I'm so sorry," says Geraldine. "She always showed such promise."

Three

_____

_____

_____

The house at Barrandov was as square-edged inside as it was out. But it was also modern in a way I had not seen before. You came in through the front door into a lobby with a corridor leading sharp right into the kitchen, which is where the maid would be. If you went straight on, you came into a living room, L-shaped, with big square windows overlooking the garden and a dining area at the far end. There was a balcony at the back, turning around the corner of the house to the northeast, looking down the hill toward the river and the old city of Prague. The great room must have been quite large, because in the center by the open staircase that led upstairs, my parents kept a grand piano.

A cabinet served as a bar, with shiny glasses, an ice bucket with a lid that was filled in the evenings, a cracked-glass mixing jug with a swizzle stick, a clutter of bottles, and Dad's soda siphon. Never a man for casual replacements, he kept these things forever. The entire floor was polished wood, which seemed unusual to me at the time; where I had come from, the floors always seemed to be creaky old planks mostly covered with worn, dusty rugs. The house, come to think of it, was a lot nicer inside than out—on an open plan, as you could find in America in the late 1950s but very rarely in England or any of the other places where we had lived.

If you jumped out the window at the end of the living room, where there was no balcony, you dropped all the way down past the basement with the spy in it, and landed by his rabbit hutch. I know because I did it once on a dare, sprained my ankle a bit, and got into serious trouble.

We kids lived mostly upstairs, which was ruled by Nanny. There was one room at each corner, laid out around a landing big enough for a table where we ate supper when my parents were out for the evening. This was most evenings now, because they were diplomats and went to a lot of parties. We did homework on this table too, and crafts. The room Nanny shared with my baby brother, Benedict, was to the right of the staircase coming up, and the bathroom to the left. The room I shared with Kate was on the far side of the landing, with two beds because we had our own beds now, mine by the door, Kate's by the window. The fourth room was Mother's and Father's. This door was usually closed, but we would be invited in sometimes, for instance when Mother was brushing Kate's hair or they were together trying on new clothes.

We had baths in the evenings, before supper was brought up, sharing the bathwater. Upstairs with Nanny, we usually ate things like poached eggs on spinach, not the roast beef or veal schnitzels we'd get at the proper dinner table when my parents were home. Ham, we learned, was considered a real treat in the Communist countries, and so we would have it sent through the Iron Curtain from a special shop in Denmark called Ostermann Petersen, along with a lot of other goods for the larder. "Where's the bloody box from Ostermann Petersen?" I would hear Mother shout. "It's late! We're doing dinner on Friday, and we have absolutely nothing!" When it came, the ham would be in a big tin shaped just like a ham hock. Communism must have been pretty tough if the Czechs had no ham and ours had to come all that way in tins.

Every day would start the same. Nanny, who was really Benedict's nanny but helped out with the two of us too, would wake us up, and while we were getting dressed and scrubbing our faces she would sit Benedict on his little chamber pot. There were no second thoughts on Victorian bowel regulation in this house, and having to go later was a terrible dread. Powdered baby milk was sent in with the Ostermann Petersen order and then mixed up in bottles by Nanny. Luckily we never seemed to be short of baby milk. Benedict had pale blond hair, just as Kate and I had had before it went dark, and he did not cry much. That was a credit to Nanny, who was good at her job. She was tiny and already seemed old to us, though she was probably no more than fifty, with grey hair and bunions on her feet. Small wonder, after pushing that big old pram for so many miles over the years.

Nelly Wright. Even I loved her, and, as Mother will tell me to this day, I was very, very bad around nannies. Nanny had been born on a smallholding, a sort of peasant farm, in a flinty part of England called Lincolnshire, where my father's family also came from. She had helped butcher the family pig as a little girl, and was put into service as a nursery maid at the local vicarage when she was ten. She told us this one Sunday morning when Kate and I woke to terrible cries from below our window. We peered out and watched as the spy downstairs, a chunky man with thick moleskin trousers, which he never seemed to clean despite stoking coal into the boiler, repeatedly whacked a rabbit's neck with the stiffened blade of his own hand. When he was done, he held it up, limp, by the hind feet. "Aye, that's the rabbit punch," said Nanny, the first to respond to our screams. "That's how you kill your rabbit. Don't feel bad—he's having it for Sunday lunch, and that's why he keeps rabbits." She was full of wisdom like this, and she was not afraid of life in Czechoslovakia because she too belonged to a time and place where rabbit hutches in back gardens had been far more prevalent than supermarkets. Once, when we were out for a walk down the path running along the ravine behind the house, we came across a woman sitting on an upturned log, cutting the heads off chickens. One by one, she held them up by the head before making a quick slice through the neck. "Aye," said Nanny. "And that's how you get your chicken to the table. Now look at 'em running around." They did too, as we craned our necks around the fence to see better, making a couple of circuits of the yard, spurting blood from their gaping necks before collapsing. Meanwhile the woman just gathered up the loose heads.

Nanny would sit Benedict on his potty and keep an eye on him as he learned to scoot it about over the floor. He could even get it over the low sill fitted in the doorway to stop the drafts, and on toward our room, chortling with satisfaction. Then Nanny would pick him up and haul him back to where he'd started from, potty and all. He had to stay on until he was finished, which, as he aged, didn't take long, at which point

Nanny would dress him up and take him over to Mother's bedroom, giving a quick rap on the door. When she said, "Come in," Nanny would put him on his stomach on the big double bed and leave them together for a while.

Benedict was learning to crawl, and he would crawl around while Mother talked to him, looking at him reflected in the mirror while she sat at her dressing table in stockings and a slip, putting on her makeup. First foundation. Then powder, applied with a puff. A squirt of scent behind the ears. A toss of her hair. Mother was a "dirty blonde" back then, a very light brown, with skin even lighter than her hair color would have suggested: she was always in danger of burning in the sun— whenever the sun actually came out in Prague—and kept a sunhat at the ready. I can still see her tossing her hair while watching Benedict in the mirror, as we looked in to say "goodbye" before running downstairs and out to the big grey Morris to be driven off to school that first winter.

Kate and I had grown up almost as twins. Her birthday was on July 2 and mine was on July 1, and so she was 364 days older, one day less than a year. That made us "Irish Twins," siblings born within the same year, as close in age as it is biologically possible to be without being true twins. Kate had simply always been there, a little bit bigger but a whole lot better. When we were very young, we both had big brown eyes and tumbles of curly hair, but Kate had a rounder face and a cupid bow to her lips, while I did not. "When you were babies in Athens," Mother would recount in a favorite story, "I was pushing you along in your double-pram one day when the Queen of Greece suddenly drove by. She had this little MG sports car, and she loved to zoom about in it, with her bodyguards absolutely screeching along trying to keep up, which made them rather cross! Well, when the queen saw you two in your pram, she stopped the car so fast that the bodyguards almost *crashed*! Anyway, she got out and came over and looked at you. She said to me, in English, 'What beautiful babies you have!' And then she drove away." This is the sort of childhood story you remember. I could always tell that Mother loved it and that we had made her proud, which was not easy.

The Kate I remember is older than that but still has a round face with a big smile of slightly snaggled front teeth. She could also look solemn and was very good at concentrating, which made her good at things like reading and sewing. Mother would teach her to work with a needle and thread when she had time, and, a bit later, how to knit. We both liked to paint with brushes and watercolors. I was good at drawing, but aside from that, Kate was better at just about everything. Sometimes, as we got older, Kate would pair up with Mother to go out for hairdos and shopping. They were happy together. But she also loved Dad, even more perhaps, and Dad was always happy to see her; they would romp around and Kate would sit on his knee. He never got angry with Kate.

In my earliest memories, even before Prague, we are getting into mischief together. Once, in Trieste, we decided we didn't want to do what we were told when Nanny Brown sent us upstairs for our afternoon rest and wanted us to put on our pajamas. Instead we pushed and shoved at the wardrobe until we moved it right in front of the bedroom door, and Nanny Brown couldn't get in to make us get into bed. She had to call Dad away from work. Another time we were playing at being surgeons, though I can't think where we got the idea from, and laid a "golliwog" on the dining room table for an operation. A golliwog was a rag doll sent as a reward for collecting Robinson's Jam vouchers; it wouldn't be socially acceptable now, as it was a caricature of a black man. In any case, we fetched the carving knife and cut it in two, right down the middle, managing to cut a gash into the polished top of the dining table in the process.

Kate would never have got involved in something like that by the time we arrived in Prague. But, then, characters in families emerge in their own ways. The last summer we were in London, we'd shared a birthday party as usual. Kate was going to be eight and I was going to be seven. Mother went to the grocery store so she could make us each a cake. New ready-made cake mixes were just coming to London from America. I got devil's food while Kate got strawberry-and-vanilla angel cake. "How very appropriate!" quipped Mother, giving that lovely giggle of hers, and we all joined in.

The odd thing is that I cannot recall a single line of dialogue with Kate. We must have spent hours and hours chatting away together. I do remember the stories we told each other in bed after lights out, though. These involved living together in an English country garden with a rockery and lots of flowers and a pond, where the sun was always out and we had a whole tribe of little kids to look after. This must have had something to do with Peter Pan and the walks we went on in Hyde Park past the famous bronze statue of him beside the serpentine boating lake. I remember Kate sitting on the end of my bed when I had the flu, reading me my favorite book, which was called *The Magic Pudding* and which no one seems ever to have heard of. I still have my copy. She helped teach me to read. I remember, too, Kate holding me while I sobbed after the first time my father beat me with a cane. It was the only time anyone ever held me after a beating.

After school we sometimes went to find Dad at the British embassy, walking through the old streets, still light because the lycée started very early and ended early. You find the embassy off an extremely narrow lane, rising steeply toward the Hrad and set securely under the Castle cliff. In fact the embassy is a bit like a castle itself, its front gateway set into a high wall topped with martial-looking crenellations. Nor is its fortified look entirely bogus; it was a medieval merchant's palace back when Prague was the seat of the Holy Roman Empire. Today the embassy building has been painted in a bright, optimistic cream color, where when I was small it was dark and dingy. Now there are elaborate security devices too, in the lane immediately in front of the gate—one of those steel barriers that swings up out of the road, presumably to fend off terrorists, and floodlights. During the Cold War the building made do with its old walls and huge wooden gates to fend off Stalin and his Communists.

"No one comes in here unless we invite them in," explained Dad, "not even the secret police. That's why we have the guards at the gate. That's why it is the British embassy. Once inside, you are in Britain." And once we were inside, it *did* feel like a refuge. We would wait at the gate while the security guard looked us over from a small stone window and telephoned Dad. Then he would open a small door set into the big one, and we would walk to the back of the yard, then up a couple of steps to another door and to his office.

One day Dad brought the car around from the embassy garage and left it running, exhaust streaming white in the fog, and Mother took the wheel while we clambered into the back. We drove to another part of town, counting the Tatras, and stopped at one of the old-fashioned apartment buildings with elaborate carvings of fat women and fruit and twirls. We were going to visit someone we kids hadn't met before, who spoke English but came from New Zealand and was named Margot Milner. She worked for the BBC, Mother said. "Margot knows a lot of people in Prague who are involved in the arts and in music," she said, "So she's going to help us find a piano teacher for Kate, and a ballet school."

And so Kate's path began to diverge from my own. She would stay at home in Prague—learning the piano and how to dance, staying in class with Monsieur Gareau, who liked her so much—while I would return to England for boarding school.

Margot Milner seemed strange to me that day. She was wearing a skirt and a short jacket in tweed, a rough material which I knew from the tweed jackets the men from the embassy wore when they were not at work, and which I would soon get myself. But it made Margo seem rough somehow, an impression that stayed with me. Her face didn't seem nearly so soft and pale as Mother's, and below her thick brown hair she had dark patches under her eyes. But she did work for the BBC, and even then that struck me as interesting. "What does working for the BBC *mean?*" I asked her. "It means telling stories over the radio," said Margot, "stories from Prague, often about people who come here to play music or act in plays." She made tea and passed around some biscuits, then arranged for another lady to teach Kate how to play the piano.

Kate would practice her scales for ages on the piano in the living room at Barrandov. While she did that I went out and played in the snow with a bunch of local boys I had met. Dad had bought a real toboggan, with big curled runners at the front like a reindeer sleigh, to replace the one he had made, though we still had that too. We had skates as well, which we used on a pond at the bottom of the hill, where I was allowed to go on my own as long as some of the older boys were there to be in charge. I was quite good at skating back then, or at least that is how I remember it. On weekends Dad took us skating on the river when the Vltava froze over, which was a great gathering time for Czechs, and where we also met other kids from the embassy. I remember there were stalls selling sausages and roast chestnuts that filled the cold, brisk air with a scent that once caught, never fades.

I have no idea how I communicated with the local boys, as I never learned more than a few words of Czech. Still, I knew perfectly well how to get into trouble. There was a traffic circle at the bottom end of the street and, just beyond, at the edge of the steep drop down to the road that took you to Prague, was a place at the Barrandov Film Studios that we called "the club." This had a bar, an empty swimming pool, and a tennis court. The club seemed to be closed, shuttered, and we would clamber over locked gates to explore. Still, we knew that sometimes there would be men inside from whom we should hide, in whatever closet or shed was nearest to hand.

One afternoon about six of us decided to climb down the cliff at the back, playing mountaineers. We got down easily enough, but halfway up again we got stuck on the fissure that formed a natural path. Suddenly one of the smallest boys froze, and the rocks started to crumble. It was the kind of fear that makes you feel hollow inside. After waiting a while, we decided to pick up the little boy and get back to the top somehow. The biggest boy had his shoulders while I had his feet. Only when we reached the top did we realize just how foolish we'd been; standing there watching us were the men we were supposed to hide from, along with two policemen who took us away to their police station. There, in a room with benches and a high wooden counter with another policeman standing behind it, looking especially fierce, they told us to sit down. I did not wet myself. But I was trembling and trying very hard not to cry. This was it! This was what happened to people behind the Iron Curtain.

An hour or more later, Dad strode into the room looking severe, if also slightly amused. The cops who had been on top of the cliff laughed now as they cuffed us around our heads, made jokes with all the parents who were coming in, and finally let us go. I didn't know quite what to think. These men were wearing uniforms with caps, for one thing, and there was nothing secret about them at all. Nor was I sure that I had really been punished. Back home I was sent straight to bed, but I wasn't beaten.

When my parents went out for parties, Mother would come into our room, where we were already tucked into bed, to say good night. She would bend over the beds to kiss each of us on the cheek, but we had to be careful not to disturb her makeup, because she would be all dressed and ready to go. One night she had on a new red evening dress that everyone said was really pretty. It had a low neck called an "empire line." When she leaned down to kiss me goodnight, I saw most of her breasts, which were very white and had been powdered. Breathing in a trace of her best perfume, I thought how much I loved my mother, and how strange it would be to be sent all the way back to England for boarding school, which wouldn't be long now.

Soon after, on a morning which must have been a weekend, we all had breakfast together. Mother was talking about the party they had just been to. It had been at Margot Milner's, and during the evening one of the many people who had been playing her piano was a man named Jiří Mucha. He had been singing as well. Apparently he had a stunningly beautiful wife, which seemed to please Mother. "They were really very interesting, don't you think?" Mother said to my father. He agreed. "Extraordinary that he has been in prison," Mother went on. *So this man has been in prison in Czechoslovakia too, I thought— just like me!* "It sounds quite awful," Mother continued. "And the wife is from Scotland! We must have them over, and get to know them."

There was a balustrade where the landing met the staircase, which turned halfway up, and if you leaned over far enough when my parents had parties of their own, you could watch the grown-ups come and go. Sometimes these parties were around our suppertime and brought a lot of people who stood around with drinks Dad made at the bar, talking loudly enough that it was perfectly clear they didn't care whether what they said was picked up by the microphone set in the floor. On other nights only a few people would come, so that everyone could be seated around the dining table, where they were served by the maid, staying late into the evening.

Kate was often allowed to go downstairs and pass around a bowl of peanuts, but I would stay upstairs—Mother said I would only misbehave—and lean over the balustrade to watch. Later, when I was a bit older, I too was allowed down to help pass around the peanuts and little crackers with cheese on them. It was very crowded, but I think I managed to acquit myself without spilling anything. Margot Milner was there, this time wearing a dress more like one of Mother's. After a while, Kate and I stopped handing around peanuts and crackers, but nobody sent me back upstairs. I remember going over to the piano, which was shut closed with glasses and ashtrays perched on top of the lid. There was also a book lying there. It featured a painting on the cover that looked as if it had come from one of the old churches we used to visit, and I stood there leafing through it. Someone would have brought it as a gift for my parents. Many of the paintings inside were horrid, I thought, with medieval-type people being flayed and tortured. Some of them showed Baby Jesus and the Virgin Mary, like at Christmas, but even more of them showed Jesus up on the cross like at Easter. There seemed to be blood everywhere.

I was trying to make sense of a painting filled with particularly complicated cruelties when a man who looked younger than the others and who seemed very friendly, almost the type you would see in the drawings that went with adventure stories, came up and talked to me. The particular picture I was studying, I remember, had Jesus on the Cross, and there were a lot of people crowded around below, several women crying, and one soldier sticking a lance into Jesus' side so that blood spattered out. On either side of Jesus was another man on a cross, but these two were hung up by having their arms twisted around the bars, and you could see on their faces how painful that was. Soldiers were bashing their knees with clubs and axes. One man even had a small devil climbing out of his head. "Who are they?" I asked the man who had walked up to me. "Them?" he answered, in an odd sort of English. "They are the malefactors."

"What's a malefactor?"

"Someone who does bad things."

I felt a strange floating feeling and my knees were folding up, and then everything went dark as I realized I was falling down onto the wooden floor. When I woke up I saw the man's face and he had his arm around me, lifting me up. Mother and Father were looking down, worried. "He'd better go upstairs," said Dad. I knew I would never be allowed down again. "I'll carry him," said the man. I felt disappointed and afraid, but I liked this man and let him carry me upstairs to our room.

Four

In summer we went cherry picking, which was a treat and a delight for everyone. It seemed odd to me that after so much cold the Czech weather could turn so warm, but Dad explained that this was because Czechoslovakia had a "continental climate," with greater extremes of temperature than when a country is by the sea, like England. Cherry trees lined the roads running straight and narrow into the countryside, and when the red cherries ripened in summer, after school had finished, the Czechs would stream out of the towns on picking expeditions because the cherries were free and for everyone. Village women with long scarves around their heads and village men with muddy boots spread out across the map with wooden carts, the bigger ones hitched to horses standing quietly, one back leg arched slightly, the hoof resting on its point, thigh muscles quivering, and tails flicking to ward off the flies. Some had brought along ladders and were able to reach even the cherries in the higher branches. Town people, too, would drive out, if they had cars, and would even catch buses.

Everyone picked as many cherries as they could, after which they spread blankets on the shoulders of the road and had picnics. It was a great gathering, like the skating on the Vltava when it froze over and everyone was friendly, their guard lowered, at least for the while.

"Czechs can't get fruit for most of the year, and they love it when they can," said Dad. "So we'll just pick enough for today." We ate ours later, Mother handing them out handful by handful and telling us not to be greedy, because too many at once would only upset our stomachs. I am not sure if I had ever eaten cherries before, because back then fruit was still seasonal in Europe, but I remember how good they tasted on that hot summer day. Just ripe, they were tart and sweet and delicious. We ate them after bread and cheese and hard-boiled eggs sprinkled with salt and tomatoes sliced in half, which was what we usually had when we drove out of Prague for a picnic. Dad brought wine in a big wicker-covered bottle he had bought in Greece and loved to use for picnics. Nanny came with us too, the three of us plus Benedict sharing the back seat.

It was a good idea to leave the city and get to know the country beyond Prague, Dad would say. He liked to see what was going on, because that was his job, even if the Communist government didn't exactly like it. Once he had driven all the way up to the mountains in the north of the country—called the Tatras, like the car—and had been arrested for "counting tanks." The Czech army soon let him go, though, because he was a diplomat. Years later he explained that he *had* in fact been counting tanks; a Russian army was moving on the border, and the Brits as well as the Americans, also on our side, wanted to find out just how big it was and what it was up to.

After picking cherries we drove out even farther into the countryside and settled in an open field with tall grass, so when you sat down you could not see over the top of it. Dad certainly wasn't counting tanks this time, as it was completely quiet, the air filled only with butterflies. Mother wore a hat against the sun, and her dark glasses. On top of the hill behind us was an old castle, much like the one in my toy box but falling down after so many years of battle and neglect. We were told it was a "ruin," and after lunch we put Benedict in his pram and set out to explore it.

Finding a bumpy path, we headed up the hill. It was quite steep, and Kate and I took over pushing the pram while Nanny followed behind us. Then we turned Benedict around so the pram handle was at the front, and I pulled it like a horse, with Kate pushing from behind. This worked well, and we got to the top well ahead of the grown-ups, laughing and sweating and out of breath. In front was a stone wall, towering over us even in its ruined state, each stone considerably bigger than the giant pram we had just hauled up. There was no one around that I can remember—no one to sell a ticket or tell us where to go. So we waited for Dad, and after we'd had some water from the cold flask he had brought up with him, he showed us the way through the gate and into the castle. We had visited castles that had drawbridges still working and great iron guards called portcullises, but all that was left of this one was the stonework. You could imagine the knights and men with bows and axes and cauldrons of boiling oil which they would pour down the walls as they fought the invaders. Dad described all this to us. In a round tower we found an iron grate set in a hole in the worn stone floor. We peered into it and saw a big room below—a cellar, maybe?—but shaped like the inside of a ball, and you could only get in through the grate we were looking through, which would be at the top of the "ball." Iron rings were set into its curved walls, and it was a long way to the bottom.

"If you went down there, how could you ever get out?" I asked.

"You *wouldn't*, unless someone pulled you out with a rope," said Dad. "It's a dungeon, where they kept prisoners. They would drop food and water down if they wanted to keep the prisoners alive. But if they didn't pull them out, they died down there." It occurred to me, suddenly, that people had always been cruel.

Later that summer Kate and I shared our last birthday party together, because after that I would be away at school, where no one celebrated birthdays. We had the party at home, and it was attended by other diplomats' children. One American family was called Timms, and I think they had three or four children, one of whom had had a birthday party where we watched Walt Disney's *Bambi*. That was the first film I had ever seen. The animals didn't seem very real, but the hunters reminded me of the spy in the basement who killed his rabbits. At our party we made do with games in the garden before sitting down for drinks and cake and singing "Happy Birthday." This might have been the first time I met the rest of the Mucha family. Jiří's son John was there, in a very baggy pair of shorts, and the odd thing is I remember him better than anyone else. The only Czech kid there, my local gang not having been invited, he spoke English just like we did. He was a year older than Kate, who was now nine, and taller than the rest of us, but he joined in the games only halfheartedly, always quiet. "Perhaps he's just shy," said Mother.

Some of my parents' new friends came to the party too, and sat and stood around chatting on the balcony that overlooked the garden. Margot Milner was among them. She was often at our house, in fact, and we often saw her when we went to see other people or to fairs or puppet shows, because she had lived in Prague for quite a while and could show Mother and my father where just about everything was.

I remember Jiří Mucha leaning over the table with a cigarette, talking softly. After a while Mother went to sit next to him, and when I ran by to fetch another toy from inside, she called me over. "Charles, say how-do-you-do to George Mucha," she said. "He's *John's* father." Jiří looked up, put his cigarette in his mouth, crinkled his eyes because of the smoke, and shook my hand. I don't think he said anything. Geraldine was sitting on the other side of the table, and I said how-do-you-do to her too. "Have you been playing with John, then?" she said, shaking my hand. She called him John with us, because we were Brits. When she was speaking Czech, however, he was Jan. I can't remember what I said by way of a response, but I do remember Geraldine tipping back her head a bit and laughing.

The next time we saw the Muchas it was on another picnic, and I think this may have been the one on the pebbly beach by a lake where Geraldine posed for that picture in her bathing suit. Indeed, either we went on a good few picnics during the heat of that summer, or there is simply something about picnics that stays in my mind. In any case, there were more people with us that next time. We spread blankets and towels by the water's edge, forgoing tables or folding chairs, though I do remember one chair with a green steel frame and green canvas, which may have been from the army. Mother and Kate both sat by Jiří as we ate, and they were talking about a book he had written after being in prison, *Living and Partly Living*. It was the first time I understood that he was a writer. The book could not be sold in Prague, apparently, because the Communists didn't like it, but it was going to be printed in English.

"I got books smuggled into the camp," Jiří was saying, comfortable as ever in the role of raconteur. "So I would be down the mine, in this very small space down in the dirt and the dark where I set up a light and read between the times I had to get up and work." It is not hard to understand how this would interest the children sitting around with their parents, plastic plates balanced precariously on their laps. Jiří seemed to shrug off his years in prison as if he were merely lighting another cigarette. He talked quietly, rolling up the sleeves of his checked shirt as the afternoon unfolded, did not eat much, and drained the wine Dad poured from the wicker-covered bottle only slowly. Jiří's job apparently had something to do with getting up from the place in the tunnel where he could read with his makeshift light, and crawling along, pushing carts filled with coal. "Of course there were many people down in that mine, you know, who were good," he went on, "and they gave me things to eat and the light so I could read. It was the guards who were stupid." Jiří often said people were "stupid," and I soon understood that this meant they were people he did not like. One of the books he had with him in the mine was a collection of Shakespeare. "Jiří read Shakespeare!" I heard Mother say. "While he was in prison! How extraordinary." Reading, she said, might well keep someone from going mad in terrible situations—something I have always kept in mind.

When we were finished with the picnic, we went swimming again in the icy lake, which at that age I didn't mind so much. Dad plunged in too, but I don't remember ever seeing Jiří in swimming shorts. Kate and I were both shivering like crazy when we got out, huddling under our towels.

Toward the end of summer we went back to London for a visit, which Mother called "going on leave." We went by air, just then becoming a popular way to get around Europe, though we still traveled quite a bit by train and by road with my father at the wheel of the Morris. The plane that flew from Prague to London was a Viscount, which had four engines with propellers and made a lot of noise. Dad sent the rest of us on ahead with Nanny, who was going to visit her family, and he followed later.

Granny was there to meet us in London, and we settled into a small hotel in Kensington. My family always stayed here, near the park with its statue of Queen Victoria and the Round Pond, where I sailed model boats with Granny.

Mother's family on both sides had all lived in China until the war, always coming home to Kensington when they were "on leave" and when they retired. Mother said it used to take weeks and weeks to get *Home*, which is how her family spoke of England, because they sailed all the way on steamships with a company called the White Star Line. She had made that journey when she was a girl, though older than I was now, because she also came Home to go to school. For the first time I got my own passport, and I knew that this was because I would now be traveling on my own the next time I went "abroad."

My father must have brought the passport with him when he came later, because I have the page with my photograph on it on one side and the date of issue with Dad's signature on the other, and I am already in my school uniform. My parents tore the page out for a keepsake when the passport expired, and Mother sent it to me not long ago when she was clearing out old files. She sent the same page from Kate's first passport too. In the photos we look like twins, though we weren't. Mother commented on that in the note she tacked on: "Such handsome children and so (at that point!) alike." The date on the official stamp of the British Embassy Consular Section Prague reads "5Sept58." Kate's reads "17Mar60," when the family left Prague altogether. For now, though, we were going our separate ways.

The first task was to get my school uniform at a big London store called Daniel Neal, which seemed to have some sort of monopoly on boarding school "kits." Mother had a list: two of everything, from the grey woolen socks, grey corduroy shorts, and grey suit with short trousers to the grey sweater with winged collar and the grey cable-knit sleeveless sweater I am wearing in the passport photograph. Shoes had numbers nailed into the soles with brass nails; I would be number 22. Daniel Neal also stocked the ties and caps that came in a different pattern for every school, schools that had been training Brits to run the empire for years. It was now 1958, of course, and the empire would be consigned to history before I was even finished with school. But I didn't know that then, and I didn't really know what to make of being sent away to school in any case. It just seemed inevitable. The list of things we were to buy included a trunk—green with wooden reinforcing bars—with my name embossed on it. I still have that trunk, though I have lost the blue Globetrotter suitcase we also bought for me to carry on the plane when later I would visit home. That had my name on it too.

From London we traveled on to a seaside town called Bexhill-on-Sea, near the tall white cliffs of England's southern coast. We stayed in a little house called a bungalow, down a quiet street with very few cars going by, and nobody talking very much. There was a lot of wind, however, which Mother called "fresh air." One morning, which would have been in mid-September, Dad took me on my own to a railway station, and we caught a train to London. I wore my new uniform and cap, buttoning the jacket, and carried my suitcase. I don't remember talking with Dad on the train, but I knew we were going to Victoria Station to catch the school train, and that we had to get there on time. When we reached Victoria there were a lot of boys all over the concourse and the platforms who also wore striped caps. Some of them were screaming and hanging on to their mothers, and I told myself that whatever happened, I would not allow myself to cry. High above us was a Victoria Station billboard, displaying caricatures of a judge in his curly white wig, an army officer in khaki, a businessman in a bowler hat, and a schoolboy in his cap. "Top People Read The Times," it proclaimed. Finally we found a platform which had a list of schools posted, including Stoke House, my destination, and my father introduced me to a tall man wearing completely round glasses with black frames. This was the headmaster. Then Dad reached into his pocket, brought out a little package, and passed it to me. "Goodbye, and good luck," he said, shaking my hand. A woman whom the headmaster introduced as Mrs. Piper, his wife, led me to a car on the train which had another sign reading Stoke House, took me to a seat and said, "Sit here." She went away, and I opened the package Dad had given me. It contained a little silver pocket knife, with one blade at each end. Like my trunk, my suitcase, and all my new clothes, it had my name on it, engraved on the side. But there was room only for the initials: CPGL. I opened the blades and ran my finger over the edges, closed them, and then stared at the initials, which kept me from having to look out the window where other boys were going by, some of them crying. Then Mrs. Piper came back with more boys, and everyone settled down in the carriage. "What's that?" asked Mrs. Piper, suddenly looking at me from across the seat.

"My Dad gave it to me!" I said. "Look, it has my initials, it's for school!"

"New boys," announced Mrs. Piper, "are not allowed penknives." She leaned forward, took it, and deposited it into her handbag.

When I returned from school the following summer, I was given my first Kodak camera for my ninth birthday. Nanny gave me a photo album to go with it, writing "with love and best wishes" on the inside of the cover. On the first page I pasted a photo of Kate standing in front of Mother's new car, a tiny white Fiat 500 from Italy, which was considered sensational because it was the only one in Prague, and very glamorous. Mother was full of fun and gaiety when she was out and about. In the picture the car is parked in front of the garage of the house in Barrandov. Kate is holding up her two favorite dolls, posing them for the snapshot as if they were real babies. The caption, written with a white crayon on the black paper they used in photo albums in those days, reads KateBridgetMinion. The car was named Minion, properly spelled as *mignon*, which means "dear little" in French, while Bridget was a doll that had once been Mother's. The other doll is standing on her own in a second snapshot, propped up against Minion's rear bumper: Angi. Kate, holding her dolls, looks like a little girl for the last time. But as you turn the pages with their black-and-white photos you can see her change.

A third photo on the first page is captioned "Muchar's [sic] Bungalow." That was Jiří's *chata*, which was quite a way outside Prague, not far from the border with Poland. Where the Russians have always had their *dacha*, the Czechs have had their *chata*, the traditional weekend cottages, often featured in literature and movies as the city dweller's dearest refuge. In the photo, Jiří's is long and narrow, made of squared-off logs above a stone foundation, with three windows on one side of an entrance porch and two on the other. Mother and Kate visited there all the time. They would set off on Friday afternoons in Mother's little car, with the roof rolled back if it was nice and sunny, Mother wrapping a scarf over her hair. Dad had bought her the car and brought it into Czechoslovakia through the Iron Curtain while I was away at school. Mother couldn't really use it when it was snowing, she told me, because it was so small that it would be dangerous. But the rest of the time, it was a joy. We all loved that car. Quite often Kate would get into it with Mother in the afternoons, when my father was still at work, and they would set off to the cobbled streets of the old town to take Kate to her piano lessons or her ballet school.

Afterward they would go to Jiří's house in the Castle Square, so Kate could play with John. To me that was the biggest change of all. Kate played with John now, rather than me, though it seemed less about *playing* than simply doing things together. The change had everything to do with me going away to school, but she was also growing up.

On the second page of the photo album is a picture of Kate standing next to John Mucha outside the *chata*, standing so close their arms are touching, and then there is another photo that shows the whole gathering, both of our families assembled together. This time the caption underneath reads: "Mummy, George, Dad, Geraldine, Kate, Nanny, John, Pig," which was our pet name for Benedict. BennyPiggy. I recall taking a picture like that at the *chata*, but the caption for this photo doesn't specify the location. It looks as if the sun would have been behind me, to the west, which would make sense, as I was taking pictures in the late afternoon before we returned to Prague, and I knew to keep the sun behind me. But it's just possible that the picture was taken outside the house in Barrandov, because that summer the Muchas often visited us there as well.

Everything turned strange that summer. When Kate wasn't with John, she was quite often seeing an even older boy called Milos, who was also Czech and who went to the same ballet class. He was much bigger than me, with thick brown hair, a long face with smaller eyes than ours, and a narrow head with a strangely flat back. I didn't like Milos. Kate and I still talked, but it was like talking across a fence. I told her about soccer and cricket and dormitories and learning Latin. Amo, amas, amat, amamus, amatis, amant. It was the first thing I had had to learn, I told Kate, and after I thought I had learned it perfectly well, the master took me out into the corridor to tell me that I would get "six of the best" if I didn't concentrate on my lessons. I told her how much "six of the best" hurt, but this time she didn't hug me. We didn't hug anymore.

Kate always got things right at school, was very good at writing and spelling, and said that Monsieur Gareau liked her so much he had asked Mother and Dad whether he could marry her when she grew up. I thought about that for a long time. Kate was only a year older than me, after all, which meant she was ten. "He said he would wait for her!" Mother said when I asked her about it.

At the end of August we went back through the Iron Curtain to Austria and stayed at a big hotel on a lake in the mountains. I have pictures of it on page three of my album. *Hotel Grand Monsea 1959.* There's a picture of Kate in the water, holding Benedict under his arms, and he looks as if he is protesting, loudly. Another one shows a ferry boat steaming away from the jetty, heading out into a landscape of trees and layered hills. It's a pretty good shot, actually. Toward the end of the holiday I fell ill at supper, at first feeling terribly hungry and then not wanting to eat anything at all. Mother felt my forehead and got angry; I had a high fever. "It's because you *wouldn't* get out of the water when you were told!" she said. "Now you're going to spoil everything!" I was sent up to bed, and soon after that a French-speaking doctor came on a house call. He said I had pneumonia and wanted to give me a shot of penicillin into my bottom. I yelled at that, refusing to turn over. "Est tu une petite fille?" he shouted back angrily. Duly ashamed, I finally turned over, and he jabbed me with the needle. Back in Prague,

I had to have three injections a day for a week or so, and was late returning to school.

When I came across the photo album years later, as I was packing up my own home to move with my kids to America, I was stunned by the photograph of the Muchas and my family outside the *chata*. The entire story is just so clear. On the left is Mother, smiling straight at the camera, with a pointy bra under her white sweater, holding Jiří Mucha's arm, one breast pressed up against his back, while Jiří, wearing one of his checked shirts, is turned slightly to the right, his arm around Kate. Kate, snuggled up into his armpit, smiles directly into the camera. Dad too is in the center of the picture, but a few steps behind, so much smaller than he had always been to me. He looks out past Kate's shoulder with Jiří's hand on it, unsmiling. Geraldine is even farther behind, in fact almost entirely hidden by Nanny. Benedict stands up against Nanny while John is on the right, holding Benedict's hand. And so there it is: Mother and Kate belong to Jiří; everyone else is out of the picture.

Children are like dogs and can tell when something is wrong. That old photograph opened the portal to old memories that had faded but never fallen still, and they are memories of my first trip to the *chata*. The plan had been for me to squeeze into the back of Minion and go with Mother and Kate to join the Muchas on Friday afternoon. Dad and Nanny and Benedict were to come up on Sunday, and we'd all drive back together with the two cars. I hadn't been there before. But I didn't want to go. I couldn't say why. I just didn't want to go.

Mother slapped me on the cheek and called Dad at the office. He would deal with me. That is what she used to say; *deal* with me. I knew perfectly well what that might mean; nevertheless I refused to climb into the car.

"Why didn't you do what your mother told you?" Dad demanded to know when he got home. "Because I feel ill," I lied. "Well, then, you had better go to bed and stay there," he said. Later, Nanny brought me soup. We went up to the *chata* in the Morris on Sunday. Jiří showed me his American car, a huge, long Chrysler that he had parked on the grass by the cottage. It was by far the biggest car I had ever seen. Mother's Minion was parked right next to it, and we joked that it could easily fit right in the Chrysler's trunk. I asked if we could go for a ride in it, but Jiří said no. "There are no parts to service it since the Communists took over," he said. "And also, it uses a lot of petrol when it does run."

Everything about Jiří was, well, impressive. We walked onto the green in front of the *chata* with buckets to get some water from the well, which was in a well house with its own door. A trout was trapped in the well, so big it could hardly turn around. "We keep it there to eat the flies and keep the water clean," said Jiří, as we carried the buckets back to the kitchen, where Mother and Geraldine were cooking.

It was a very small house. "Where do you and Mother and John and Geraldine sleep?" I asked Kate. She looked away, pointed to a boxy wooden bed with a makeshift curtain, and said that John slept there. But she wouldn't say any more, and what I remember most is wondering why Kate would no longer talk to me.

Five

The last time I saw Prague as a boy, it was dripping with the same winter fogs and ice as when we had arrived, its medieval spires soaring dark against the skies. There was the same scent of roasting chestnuts when we walked across the Charles Bridge and the narrow streets to the fair that had been set up in the Old Town Square. I had returned for the Christmas holidays of 1959. We had three weeks off, and as the Foreign Office would pay for children to return for two of the three school breaks, I would fly back to Prague for Christmas and the summer. We drove in from the airport with the chains on the Morris chattering, and the first thing I did after saying hello to Kate and Benedict was to find my Kodak, as cameras were not allowed at school.

No Muchas show up in the snaps I took over this vacation. There is one of Kate in her snow clothes, looking grown up as she poses, chin in hand, smiling but with her mouth closed. In another she looks a younger girl again, holding up her doll, Angie, spelt with an "e" on the end this time, which suggests that I must have been learning something at school. Kate, whose holiday at the lycée was shorter than mine, still went off with Dad in the mornings, carrying her little leather satchel, and sometimes went on to ballet in the afternoons. Monsieur Gareau clearly had not been allowed to marry her but remained her teacher. Milos was still her friend at ballet, and I remember that John Mucha occasionally came to our house. Sometimes Mother would drive Kate to see John at the Muchas' house as they used to do, but not as often. We all went to a Christmas party there. But there are no Muchas in the Christmas photos I took, lining everyone up outside the house after the big lunch, before it got too dark. In one, Dad and Mother stand behind Nanny and Benedict, bigger now, and Kate is slightly apart, no one's arm around her this time, hands clasped together loosely in front of her. Mother looks down at the ground, hands brought together at her bosom, a whimsical look on her face if you look closely, while Dad, in turn, looks down at her, hands behind his back. Margot Milner is standing to the left, also clasping her hands in front of her. "Margot is lonely on her own at Christmas," Mother had said.

They packed up the house at Barrandov at the end of March and sold Mother's Fiat for a good price because it was the only one in Prague, and Dad sent the rest of the family on ahead to England. They would soon be on their way to Egypt for Dad's next posting. By Easter they were all installed in a house in Surrey, south of London, which Granny had borrowed for them from some friends called Brown. When I got there from school on the spring break, they were already settled in. Granny showed me the house on the other side of the garden fence and told me that it was the home of a famous man called Barnes Wallis, who during the war had invented the "bouncing bomb." Granny greeted his wife, who was pottering about outside the greenhouse, with a "hello." How fantastic to be staying next to Barnes Wallis, the "boffin"! I knew all about him, because the third movie I ever saw was *The Dambusters*, which told the story of his bomb and how it had enabled the RAF to smash German dams, thus helping win the war. Once, I even caught a glimpse of him. I didn't much like going up to bed at the house in Surrey, with its dark creaky wood and the enormous crucifix hanging on the wall just above the landing where the stairs turned. There are not many of these statues of Jesus on his cross in English houses, and after Prague I did not like them at all. I learned to run up the stairs with my right hand over my face like a coach horse's blinker—anything to avoid looking at that holy horror. In the bedroom I shared with Kate, everything was dark too, all the furniture. There was a great, heavy wardrobe with a mirrored door, and every morning when we got up, then every night when we went to bed, Kate stood sideways before that mirror in her pajamas and looked at herself, stroking her tummy downward in a sort of slashing motion as she said to herself: "Slim, slim, slim. Must lose weight. No potatoes, no bread, no fat. Slim, slim, slim."

Those are the words I remember her saying. I remember them one by one. Over and over again. For the fact was, Kate had been stricken with anorexia, though the doctors would not tell Mother and my father that for another eighteen months or so, when she first collapsed from starvation.

Anorexia nervosa. At the time we mostly called it "slimmer's disease." But Mother, at least early on, said Kate was simply losing her puppy fat because she was going to change from a girl to a woman. I had no idea what that meant, except that Kate would be getting bigger; but then so would I. Actually Kate never did get any bigger, because it turned out she had "slimmer's disease" really badly, and so she never grew. We still played around together when we were at the house in Surrey, played cards and sailed little wooden boats I had whittled on the lily pond they had there. But by the time I got to Cairo for the summer holidays, Kate was eleven and looked entirely different. She wore grown-up dresses with tight cinched waists, and her hair was longer but somehow thinner too, limp even when she hadn't combed it. She hardly talked anymore, always fretting over her lessons, except, that is, when she was arguing with Mother and Dad at meals because she wasn't hungry. These arguments were beginning to happen all the time. They were increasingly nasty too, with a great deal of shouting. First my parents would lose their tempers with Kate, then with each other. Nanny would take Benedict back to her room while Saleem, the butler, would anxiously bring jugs of fresh lemonade he had made onto the veranda. It was the most delicious lemonade I had ever tasted; still, Kate would drink only a sip. Saleem asked if she wanted it with more sugar, but she always said, "No, thank you," very politely. Dad fired the cook some time later, but that was mainly because Mother caught him smoking hashish outside the kitchen and thought he was lazy. He had sores on his feet too.

Mother thought that maybe the climate didn't suit Kate. "It's too bloody hot," she would say. "I'm allergic to that sun. If it catches me, I swell up like a strawberry." She wore long sleeves and stayed under the umbrella. Kate didn't complain, but she didn't want to do anything either.

For my part, I loved being in Cairo. Most mornings we rose as it was getting light and was not so hot and drove to the stables right under the Great Pyramids to go riding through the desert. After I learned to ride properly, the grooms—who wore dishdashes (long one-piece tunics) and could gallop up the sandy wadis without even wearing boots—let me ride a grey stallion called Nimr, which meant Tiger. You had to hold him on the bit, but he was the fastest horse in the stable. Once, we went for a long night ride under the full moon to the Old Pyramids at Gazira. Mother put on a party in a tent when we got there, with great dishes of meat on skewers and flat bread, and there was a camel to ride. People always loved Mother's parties. In the afternoons we would go swimming at a pool in a private club. And then sometimes we went out at sunset on the Nile in an ancient sailing boat, called a farouk. Mother would wear white trousers and a striped shirt and her sunglasses with white rims, looking to me like an American movie star. Those jaunts always put her in a good mood, and she would break out a set of bongo drums to smack with abandon.

I loved Cairo, but Kate, it seemed, just wanted to read books. Then it was time for me to go back to school again while Kate stayed on. I wouldn't see her until the next summer holidays, because it was a long way to Cairo, and the Foreign Office would pay for only one air ticket a year. That meant that when I eventually did see Kate, I was in for a shock. Her condition had only grown worse.

Soon after I flew back to school again, the doctors in Cairo decided that they could do no more for Kate, and that she would have to go into the hospital there or back in London. By now she was twelve and weighed just seventy-two pounds.

She had a sore at the base of her spine because she had to spend much of her time in bed, her emaciated limbs chafing against the cotton sheets. Mother flew her back to London, where she was taken to a hospital called the Royal Free, or maybe it was St. Bartholemew's first and then the Royal Free. The nurses snaked tubes down her nose and into her stomach; they might not be able to make her eat, but they kept her alive. Her face by now looked as if someone had sucked it dry from the inside. Meanwhile Mother took a studio in Kensington, which had a gas hotplate for cooking like the one I would see so many years later in Geraldine's room. We would put coins in a meter whenever we wanted to heat a can of food, or boil some eggs, or light the fire to get warm.

It is easier to bury secrets in children than it is to keep the secrets from them. Truth has a way of percolating in, and you know, even when you can't *quite* know. Something had happened in Prague, and it had something to do with why Kate was now in the hospital, where you could go to see her only at teatime, and why I was staying with Mother in a single rented room with a camp cot on the floor for me and a bathroom down the hall. It was quite a while before I saw Mother all dressed up again, too.

Keeping up with all that was going on in the family became more difficult because I was away at school most of the time, and I never did get back to Cairo, to that lovely veranda overlooking the Nile, or to that horse named Nimr. Mother and Kate came and went. I would hear about it in the letters Mother sent me once a week. They must have been back in Cairo by Christmas, because Granny took me to stay with my uncle's family, and my cousins were clearly annoyed at having another boy by the Christmas tree. But Kate just started "slimming" all over again, and by Easter she was back in the London hospital. Mother returned to a room in Kensington, and I spent quite a few days with her there. She was lonely and talked to me. A psychiatrist, she told me, had suggested that maybe Kate had simply not wanted to grow up when the time came, and by starving she was effectively stopping herself from growing up.

"It's called the 'Peter Pan syndrome,'" Mother explained. "After all, Peter Pan didn't want to grow up either."

But Kate herself would not say.

"The trouble is," said Mother, "the doctors obviously haven't got a clue what to *do* about it."

"Maybe Kate's worried that if she grows up she'll have to marry Monsieur Gareau after all," I suggested, trying, in a way, to be funny. Gareau was a creep, we agreed, with his green ink and all that, but Mother pronounced him "really quite harmless," not to mention a good teacher.

"He still writes to Kate, you know," said Mother. "He even sent her a Christmas card."

It must have been early in the summer that Dad finally left the embassy and returned to London, as otherwise I would have had another holiday in Cairo. He should have been in Cairo for another year. Every so often diplomats do come back to headquarters before they are through with a posting, but it is almost never a good thing. The Foreign Office, which my parents called simply "the Office," is on Whitehall, across the green from Big Ben and the houses of Parliament, between the Home Office, No. 10 Downing Street, and the Admiralty.

Once, of course, Britain had run the empire from Whitehall, where now it ran only itself.

Dad was coming back, my parents explained, because it was too difficult being in Cairo with Kate needing to go into the hospital so often; it would be better to be Home. But now that I was twelve, it was obvious from the things I heard, particularly when my parents were having a row, that there was much more to the story—that their being back in London had something to do with the way they had been such good friends with Jiří Mucha. Apparently there were people in the Office who thought that Jiří might have been a spy. A spy! That sounded to me a bit like the man in the basement, but Mother would have none of it. "Whatever George might have been," she snapped, "he was not like the man in the basement." My father, however, was always very careful about what he said in front of the family. Later, after I became a newspaper reporter—running after the wars as Jiří had done when he worked for the BBC, before going back to his palace in Prague—he would be particularly careful what he said in front of me.

Dad rented us a house in another part of Surrey from the Browns' house, and took the train to the Office every morning, like everyone else, which seemed strange to me. It was a small Georgian farm house, the fields of which had been sold to make a council estate, which Americans would call subsidized housing. But that spread of houses over the fields meant that my parents could afford to rent the house, which was close enough to the railway station for my father to begin his daily journey on a bicycle. Each morning he put a clip on the right leg of his suit trousers to protect the cuff from the oily chain, and, looking even taller than usual when he swung that leg over the bike's high, old-fashioned saddle, pedaled away. He carried a raincoat in case of rain, and a tweed cap which he kept in its pocket.

I stayed in a small room over the kitchen at the back, the part of the house dating from the 1400s. The floor here was sloped and narrow, but Mother had put a bookshelf there with all of my old books, and had hung a print of Van Gogh's sunflowers right over the bed, which cheered things up a bit. Next to me was a spare room where people would come and stay, which they did often, for my parents still saw a lot of friends. The rest of the family had rooms in the front of the house—the kind of square, light rooms the Georgians were well known for building.

After a while Nanny was "let go," and she retired back to her village in Lincolnshire. Mother looked after Benedict for the three years or so before he too went off to boarding school. The family kept in touch with Nanny Wright for years until she died, but I never saw her again. Kate, determined to get top marks, spent nearly all her time in her room, reading and working at her lessons, even during the holidays. She knew that would please Dad, who had always won scholarships. But it was a fine line between discouraging one habit and encouraging another. Mother would go through Kate's drawers and find food she had hidden away so that no one would know she hadn't eaten it. Then everyone would get upset, and there would be a row. Later, Dad would come home and go to Kate's room, sit on the bed with her and hold her, speaking to her quietly. We knew he loved her more than anyone, and that she felt just the same, and Dad got sadder and sadder as we grew up because the one thing Kate could not give him was to get better.

People at the Office were asking about what Mother started to refer to as "the affair." My parents were in some sort of trouble, it seemed, and would be until the Office was certain that Jiří had not learned secrets that he could pass along to the Czech secret police. I understood now that "the affair" had been a love affair, that Jiří had taken Mother away from my father for a while. I was learning about sex now, and began to see Mother differently. I remember how much I admired her when she was all dressed up to go to parties, how exciting it was to hear her laugh, and how happy she seemed.

Mother had always set Dad up as an example, but now he seemed very distant. Indeed, for a long time I did not even like him. "Your father won a scholarship to Radley," Mother said, "and look at you! Mr. Piper says you probably won't even pass the exam to get into Radley at all, and that means we are going to have to find another school." What did I care if I didn't follow in my father's sainted footsteps? How much nicer to be like Jiří, smoking cigarettes and having affairs. No one ever sat down and explained the whole predicament to me. You could not have expected them to. So how did I know so much? How, for instance, did I know that a man called Charles Elwell, who talked to Mother about Jiří, came from MI5? I had already learned that MI5 was about spies, and how perilous that world of secrets and double-cross could be. There was a story running in the newspapers at the time about British and American traitors who had given Stalin and his Communists the secret of the atomic bomb after the war, and were now being caught one by one. Two Brits had run away to Russia, and everyone was sure there were more. It was a story known as the Third Man. Then the James Bond movies came out and captured just about everyone's imagination. Bond was a spy who actually fought other spies and villains, and had great adventures doing it. He also had love affairs. Once, my father met me at Victoria Station on his way back from work and took me to see *Goldfinger*. It was wonderful to see him laughing, and we had a great time that evening. Afterward he confided that there was an SIS, which stood for Secret Intelligence Service, but added that spies were not really like James Bond. And you could tell that he knew.

Mother would say things that were like pieces in a jigsaw puzzle. I liked to sit on a kitchen stool and watch her cook when I was home from boarding school. I would vacuum the dining room floor for her too. Mother, meanwhile, would say things like: "Of course, George will never divorce Geraldine." Which must have had something to do with Geraldine being beautiful. There was no question of my parents' getting divorced either, despite all the rows. Dad was the love of Mother's life despite everything, she always said, and Dad's career would surely be ruined if they were ever to divorce. They couldn't imagine not being diplomats, with all the parties and what Mother called "prestige." Later, in 1967, when my parents were finally abroad again with my father back on the Cold War front lines in Berlin, Mother said: "What would break my heart is if George had the affair with me because he was told to and not because he wanted to." We had been driving through Berlin in Mother's new white sports car, an MG with spoked wheels and a great sound when she went fast, and I had only recently found out that Jiří had stayed in my family's house in Berlin while my father was away learning German. It was hard to know what to make of this, though by this time I had grown used to

Mother's stories and grateful for the moments when I had her confidence. Once, when I was walking home in the early hours from the bars in the Kreutzberg, where student rebels and hippies would gather, I saw Mother's white MG parked outside a night club called the Black Bottom. The doorman wouldn't let me in.

The fact was, my parents had never really lost touch with their problematic friends from Prague. Margot Milner came to stay one night in the house in Surrey, and on another occasion so did Jiří, which surprised me. This was in about 1964, when I would have been fourteen. He drove up in a Saab, which he had driven through the Iron Curtain, and this was interesting because I was familiar with the model and knew it to be Swedish. I had always assumed that Jiří was trapped behind the Iron Curtain. How could he have driven a Swedish car to the West?

Mother made supper, and we all sat around the dining table. Kate was there too, though she wouldn't eat and got away with it because no one wanted a row while Jiří was there. "When I drove through the border to Vienna," Jiří said, slumped nonchalantly in his chair as usual, "the guards spent a long time looking at my papers, because they would not believe that I had a valid visa to leave the country. But I did!" It was okay in those days to smoke after the main course, though not cigars, and Mother put ashtrays on the table.

"Then they started to search the car. They looked under the seats, at the engine, which is at the back of the Saab, and in the trunk, which is at the front. Then, finally, they waved me through." Jiří paused for effect, drawing in tobacco smoke. "They were too stupid to look under the luggage in the trunk, which is where the engine should be! And *that* was where I had hidden my father's paintings!" The story made Jiří sound like James Bond himself. He wasn't on a mission to assassinate a villain or save the world, as far as I knew, but he had sneaked past the border guards to sell his father's paintings to the West, which ultimately would launch the whole new fashion for Alphonse Mucha. On this first trip beyond the Iron Curtain, Jiří slept in the small narrow room next to mine, and I could hear him cough into the night from all the cigarettes he smoked.

In Surrey the family settled into a routine of sorts. I, and later also my brother, would be away at school and back for the holidays. Meanwhile Father went to the Office every day, and Kate to a day school for girls. Then, every summer after exams, she would collapse and return to the hospital, where they would put the tubes through her nose and restore her weight. This fattening-up would last until the end of school the next year, at which point she would collapse all over again.

There was sadness in the house, so it was good to be out on a bicycle, and I often went fishing. Sometimes I went with a friend and we would get hold of a girlie magazine. Waiting for the fish to bite, we would stare with longing at photos of hips and waists and breasts with big pink nipples.

One time I went to visit Kate in the hospital with Mother, and waited while Mother went to talk with the doctor. "Bloody man!" she said when we were driving home. "He spent the entire time asking me questions about Kate's life at home, as if the whole thing was *my* fault!"

The theory at home was that maybe Kate had always been "too sensitive." Some people, Mother thought, were just born like that. "Maybe it would have been better if we had sent her home to school when you went," she said. "Oh, well—one can't do anything right. . . ." Another of her favorite expressions was: "Oh, well—punished for our sins."

When my parents went to Berlin, Kate enrolled at a training college for teachers. Everyone hoped that she might settle down as a teacher and learn to cope with life now that she was almost grown up. Those hopes were soon dashed, however. It wasn't long before she was back in the hospital, and this time she ended up in a large hospital for mental patients. I was at university when I went to visit her there. At first, the hospital, set amid acres of green grass and trimmed trees, with tall white windows marching evenly along long walls made of red brick, looked like a country mansion or a college campus. But as soon as you walked up the flagstone stairs to the front door, you knew this was a place of waste and despair. After signing in with a nurse, I was sent down a series of long corridors, all painted that pervasive stale green of British public buildings of the day, turning this way and that, and the people I passed had their eyes turned to a hidden past, until finally I found Kate's ward.

Kate was pleased to see me and, taking me by her skinny little cold hand, led me to the cafeteria. She insisted that I have some tea, said I was looking thin, wanted to know if I was eating enough at school. But after that, neither of us could think of much to say. Even the cafeteria smelled of urine. After an hour or so, I left her there, waving goodbye. Kate never really left the hospital again.

After I left university and cut my hair, and got a real job on my first newspaper, my parents began to leave my telephone numbers as an emergency contact for the hospitals. Soon after starting my job, I was sent to Sheffield in the north of England, where they used to make steel, to complete a course for journalists on law, government, and how to take notes in shorthand. Near the end of it, a secretary came into the class and whispered in my ear that I had to take a call. Kate had swallowed a whole bottle of aspirin, I was told, and the hospital was worried that she was dying; her stomach—or what was left of it after all those years of starving—was burned out and bleeding. I had a car and drove back down, as fast as I could, in three hours. Kate was still alive when I got there, and I hurried down those stale green corridors to the emergency ward, pushing deeper and deeper into my own sense of dread.

Kate was lying on a gurney with tubes everywhere, naked, just a bag of bones under a blue sheet stained with blood. "Thank God, you're here!" the nurse said. "We think she might pull through, but she's critical." And then she said: "I'm exhausted. Would you mind terribly staying here with her while I go for some tea? Now, if her nose turns blue, you'll just need to press that red button over there as quickly as you can." Alone in the windowless hospital room, I sat down on a stool by the gurney, staring at Kate lying so still, and then I saw her nose turn blue. "Shall I just let you go?" I asked.

She had suffered for years, tormented. She wanted to die. She'd had enough. And all she had left was this dreary, lonely hospital. I leaned over her, close to her face. I paused. And then I turned around and pushed the button hard with my finger. I hadn't had the courage.

The nurse ran back with doctors now, and a lot of frantic orders were shouted back and forth. They pulled at tubes and pushed at tubes. And moments later the screen on the heart monitor showed that they had saved Kate once again. She breathed with a broken rhythm.

After that Kate stayed alive, but she could never really eat properly again because of the damage to her stomach, which, in a way, made the anorexia irrelevant. Her brain had been damaged in the process, however, and she began to black out with fits that were not unlike epilepsy. I saw her less and less now, visiting once a year or so, and, when I was grown up enough to have a house, driving her back to my home for the day. She came to my first wedding, which was in a church, though not to my second. She even came to the christenings of my children in a chapel in London's St. Paul's Cathedral, where my children were christened because by then my father had been knighted for his diplomatic work, Sir Peter, and knights had a private chapel they could use for family events. Both times Mother brought the christening dress that three generations of our family had used. But after the services Kate wouldn't get out of the car for the receptions because she couldn't face the crowd. As her mind deteriorated further, she could remember my daughter but not my son, who came later. Finally my father helped find her a home where she could settle and be comfortable, a home for people with epilepsy.

There Kate made friends with a fellow patient whose name was Andrew, and in his own way he fell in love with the ruins of my sister. She had always had that draw; even when we were just kids, everyone who crossed our paths wanted Kate. Andrew came from a good family somewhere in Scotland, so even Mother was pleased. When you went to visit, you would see them tottering around together, with crash helmets on their heads just in case they had a fit and fell over. They were content, and it was one of those miracles.

One Sunday in April 2000 I was back in London from New York and my parents, old and retired, were up from their house in the country, and so we met at their club for lunch. The dining room tab in these gentlemen's clubs is on account, so when a waiter came up and whispered in my father's ear—just as the secretary had done in mine in that journalism class—he could just drop his knife and fork and run to the garage. Kate, he had been told, was lying unconscious in the hospital emergency room. Dad was seventy-six, and his sight was fading a bit and his reactions slowing, but he drove like a cop with his siren going, knocking over a traffic cone and nearly hitting a traffic bollard. After pulling up to the hospital, he ran in and called out in his strongest voice for a nurse to take him to Kate's bed. Then, diving behind the curtain, he bent over her and held her. He sat on one side of her bed that night, holding her hand, while Mother sat on the other.

We buried Kate a few days later in the churchyard in the village where my parents lived. Crows had long ago colonized a rookery in the trees that grew among the graves, and there were dozens of them, big and black. They flew up and circled when we marched in with her child-sized coffin, and cawed, loud as fury. They drowned the preacher's every platitude.

Six

It was after Kate died that I began to think again about Prague.
Childhood memories nag, and some won't go away. Those
few years we spent as companions had long since passed, but
when I went to put flowers on her grave I felt close to her once
again. For the first time since she had sunk into darkness, I was
able to conjure her face without flinching. And then other images would surface, some of them prompting love and others
simply puzzlement.

I had moved far from home, working as a journalist in New
York, but once a year I would fly back to England with my own
kids for a family visit. Spring was a good time as the airfares
were low and my father's garden would just be sprouting cro-
cuses and daffodils and apple blossoms. We would walk down
Devon lanes squeezed between hedges alive with birds' nests
and rabbits, and across the cow field to the churchyard in boots
weighed down by mud. After a couple of years the lichens began to welcome Kate's tombstone to the past and its comforts.
The crows still rose and circled, but calmly.

Mother was in her seventies now, all the old romances quieted into nostalgic afterglow. Sometimes as he aged, my father's anger would surface. "Dreadful mistake, marrying that woman!" he blurted out a few times. Once he would have laced on his old hobnailed army boots and left for a five- or ten-mile walk before returning home for a silent supper. Now he just stormed out into his garden. But they had settled into a sort of ease. We would go out to dinner to celebrate the ever-climbing numbers of their wedding anniversaries, for they had been married in April. On a fine warm day one year we went to picnic on Dartmoor, open country to the south of the village. Still fit, Father clambered up rocks with my son and then settled on the blanket to pour wine.

I knew that it was up here on this moor that my mother had last met with Charles Elwell from MI5, and they too had picnicked. She had been cross about it afterward. "It's all so tedious," she had said. "It happened so long ago! What more does he want?" That must have been back in 1971 or '72, when my parents bought their first house in the country, and Mother often stayed there alone. "And the most extraordinary thing happened," she had continued. "In the middle of the picnic, he made a pass at me! Lunged! It was awful." She had brushed him off and then taken him to the station for the train back to London. What had Elwell wanted? Her? Or was he still digging into Prague, more than ten years later, and testing? Jiří Mucha's obituaries later recorded him as laughing at the rumors that he had been a spy, and thus dismissing them. Elwell, however, seemed unconvinced.

In my fifties, growing older and working less, with time to spare for the first time in years, I started to search my newspaper library, and I found a folder with a few old clips, long ago turned brown. There was the obituary, with a thumbnail portrait of Jiří, eyes heavy-lidded as ever, cigarette held loosely between his fingers. He looked like a hawk, lazily at rest. But there was not much else. His name had come up a few times in articles about the Art Nouveau revival of the 1960s, circled in blue by the librarians as they clipped and filed. He would be presented as "the son-of-Alphonse," who had arranged this exhibition or that book. One story followed a dispute over ownership of a Mucha painting put up for sale in Chicago. He surfaced too as a liberation hero around 1968, when it looked as if Czechoslovakia might throw off the Soviet yoke. Amazingly, not long after Russian tanks had rolled in to put an end to the so-called Prague Spring, Jiří was reported having lunch with Kenneth Tynan, the British theatre critic who staged the raunchy review *Oh! Calcutta!*, a celebrated hit in both London and New York. Jiří had been in London for the publication, at last, of his gulag memoir, *Living and Partly Living*. Tynan then wrote a feature for the *Los Angeles Times*, headlined "The Arts and the Czech Crises." "Up to Sept. 8," Tynan wrote, "Mucha knew of no artists who were under arrest." Jiří figured the Soviet invasion had been the work of old-guard Commie plotters and accused the London literati of failing to stand up for their Czech friends. "Where was your protest?" he asked. In 1969 Jiří himself wrote an essay for the *New York Review of Books*, blaming Czech Communists for being a "fifth column" for the Russians, which he said he had had to smuggle out to the West. "All the old, discarded, venomous, cruel and discredited officials who under the previous regime held their posts for services rendered as informers and ruthless brainwashers," he wrote, "are creeping into the open and getting ready for a makeover." The trail of library cuttings went cold.

I had once loved the spy novels of Graham Greene and John le Carré. Deeds of betrayal took place in darkened woods in le Carré's Czechoslovakia, which his characters called "Czecho," and which felt strangely true to the country I remembered. And I learned from his fictional spymaster to follow the links from one name to the next. So perhaps, I thought, I might find more information if I looked up the name of Margot Milner. It had been Margot, after all, who must have introduced Mother to Jiří. One quiet afternoon I got around to punching up Google on the laptop and tapped in: Margot Milner. Screeds of Margots and Milners came up, but none of them the BBC correspondent I was looking for. So I tapped in: Margot Milner Prague. More screeds flowed down the screen, much of it the same material I had just scrolled past. This time I pushed on, though, page after page, scanning for names in bold with half-focused eyes. And then I stopped at one headline: "An Australian Communist in Prague," which was linked to a newspaper or magazine called *The Hummer*. No immediate sign of *Margot* or *Milner*, but *Communist* was interesting, so I kept on clicking with the computer mouse. "The Hummer," I read. "Publication of the Sydney Branch, Australian Society for the Study of Labour History. An Australian Communist in Prague. By Philip Deery." In the very first paragraph I found this reference: "Little is known and even less is written about those who lived outside Australia, especially in 'the socialist sixth of the world' or behind 'the Iron Curtain.' Perhaps the only Australian equivalent of, for example, John Reed or Herman Field, is Ian *Milner*—and he left no memoirs. When we do find snippets of such experiences, they represent an interesting footnote to the history of Australian communism." This certainly caught my attention. John Reed, after all, was the American Communist leader who, after writing an eyewitness account of the Russian Revolution called *Ten Days That Shook the World*, lived in exile in Moscow and was later portrayed in the Hollywood movie *Reds* by Warren Beatty.

The main character in Deery's account is Stephen Murray-Smith, a crusty old Communist traveling through Europe and writing nonsense like this: "Decadent aspects of W. European civilization have penetrated far into Czech life, and Prague is still a surprisingly bourgeois city." He lived in Prague from June 1949 to April 1951, and among the "small community of left-wing Australians" he found "Ian and Margot Milner." *Margot Milner*! It was news to me, of course, that she was married, for I had never met a Mr. Milner. I wondered now where I might find Margot, or whether she too had died. The last time she had come up in the family gossip, Mother had talked of her living in London, retired from the BBC. They had lost touch, however. I went back to the newspaper morgues, looking for death notices or an obituary. And there was one, just one, in London's *Independent*: "Margot Leigh Milner. Born in New Zealand in 1911, died in London, 1995." The second paragraph read: "As the first wife of Ian Milner, a translator and scholar who became Professor of English at Charles University in Prague, she suffered from the allegations of espionage leveled against him by the Australian authorities in the Petrov case in 1954, when Vladimir Petrov defected to Australia, claiming to be a KGB agent. She had urged her husband to return to face the charges, but he declined and instead submitted a defense through the British Embassy in Prague which has never been properly considered from that day to this." The next paragraph complains that his story "highlighted the basic injustice of the means whereby the charges were leveled, whatever the eventual outcome. Margot Milner showed unceasing loyalty to her husband, although the defection of Kim Philby and the way in which he had deceived his wife caused her heart-searching reflections."

In other words, Milner *might* have been a defector like Philby, but if he was, Margot would not have known. Hardly the sort of tribute usually found in an obituary. In a le Carré spy novel, though, the obituary itself might have been serving as a covert intelligence signal. Petrov, the Russian who seemed to have implicated Milner, was only "claiming" to be a KGB defector, according to this writer. On the other hand, it is well known that Philby, who had prompted Margot's "heart-searching," was Britain's infamous Cold War traitor, the MI6 secret service officer who rose to the top while all along "feeding" the KGB. Dozens of undercover agents had died at his word. Philby was the Mole, the loathsome traitor burrowing in the ranks, the Third Man. It was he who had tipped off Guy Burgess and Donald Maclean, British diplomats reporting to Moscow from Washington, so they could escape to Russia as the net closed in. After which Philby too eventually defected "home" to his Soviet masters.

The obituary seemed to suggest that Milner was a traitor and defector like Philby, even as it denied it. But then it offered another reason for Milner to have settled amid the fear and relative deprivation of Soviet Prague: "Margot had developed considerably as a pianist but severe osteoarthritis began to affect her fingers. Her husband recommended treatment in the famed Czech spas, and so they left for Prague." Surely the idea that a couple would choose to live amid Communist terror for the sake of a spa treatment was stretching credulity. More to the point, perhaps, was the obituary's revelation that before she married Milner in 1940, Margot's social conscience had prompted her to raise funds for the victims of the Japanese invasion of China at the start of the war. "She joined the Communist Party," it observed, "and trained as an ambulance driver."

Clearly there was more to Margot Milner than the piano-playing correspondent in Prague, the lonely expatriate guiding newly arrived diplomats and holding parties to introduce them to the locals. Reading this, I felt the thrill of the chase, or at least a tingle of it. I trolled some more and came up with a 1941 photograph from the National Library of New Zealand: Ian and Margot Milner, on a deserted beach near Victoria, Australia. The wind is blowing and, though Margot is a slender thirty here, I see right away that this is the same woman I photographed seventeen years later. Wearing khaki shorts and a light-colored sweater over a crisp Oxford shirt with a pointed collar, she looks straight at the lens, giving us a full, toothy smile, her arms folded below her breasts. Milner has his right arm around her, his fingers gripped around her right arm. He is wearing a sleeveless pullover tucked into baggy jungle shorts, a style of dress nerdy even when I was a child. Whatever he had been, Ian Milner was no James Bond. He has a narrow face, very English, with a high brow, and the thick hair blowing in the wind has already begun to recede. As to why such an apparently innocuous personal snapshot would be held in the national library, the site offered no explanation.

Now I went back to search for Ian Milner, clicking on a file headed Australian Security Intelligence Organisation, ASIO, from an information service named SourceWatch. It told me that in 1949 something called the "VENONA project" had "uncovered sensitive British and Australian government data being transmitted through Soviet diplomatic channels." VENONA was the "joint code-breaking operation run by the United States and the United Kingdom from 1943 to 1949." Milner came up in the next paragraph: "Among MI5's and ASIO's main suspects were Wally Clayton, a prominent member of the Australian Communist Party, and two diplomats with Australia's Department of External Affairs, Jim Hill and Ian Milner." Then SourceWatch got to the Petrov Affair: the Australian spy catchers were "instrumental in arranging the defection of Vladimir Petrov, Third Secretary of the Soviet Embassy in Australia. Two weeks later, his wife, also an intelligence officer at the embassy, was sensationally seized from the Soviet MVD by ASIO officers when their plane stopped for refueling in Darwin." That prompted a royal commission. It concluded that Petrov and his wife *were* the real thing after all, KGB defectors, that they were "truthful witnesses," and that "the only Australians who knowingly assisted Soviet espionage were Communists."

VENONA had caught the atom spies, the American traitors who had given Stalin the secrets to the atomic bomb. It had done so by listening to messages from Russian embassies to KGB headquarters, and cracking code names, thus proving

Klaus Fuchs to be the scientist who leaked the blueprints for the bomb, and identifying Julius and Ethel Rosenberg as his couriers. All three went to the electric chair. Then VENONA uncovered Burgess and Maclean, and picked up signals from the Third Man, though the code-breakers never could put Philby's face to the name. Searching for the name "Milner" had, it seemed, led me straight to the greatest spy story of the Cold War. But I still did not know where "main suspect" Milner fitted in, let alone Jiří or my mother.

After the Australian VENONA records were declassified in America in 1996, an Australian academic named Frank Cain drew on them to produce a history of the scandal that in Australia seems to have become known simply as "The Case." At the end of 1946, Cain writes, Milner had resigned from the External Affairs Department and taken a job in New York with the United Nations Secretariat. Jim Hill was still working with External Affairs at the time while Wally Clayton, the third of the original suspects, functioned as "spymaster." The head of External Affairs, Cain wrote, sent Hill to London "for interrogation by the famous W. J. (Jim) Skardon, who, six months previously, had obtained a confession from the atomic spy, Klaus Fuchs." Sure that Hill would break, ASIO prepared to pounce on the other suspects and persuade them to confess too. But it all went wrong. "Hill remained silent and was sent back to Canberra, then later transferred to legal work in the Attorney-General's Department." A paragraph later, Cain writes: "Ian Milner unexpectedly returned to Australia, with his wife Margot, on leave from his UN position, in September and October 1949 and was subject to close ASIO surveillance, although nothing incriminating was observed." All of them escaped prosecution. The royal commission "did condemn Milner, and hinted that they had seen the US material." By this time, however, Milner had already defected to Prague.

I mulled the scenario—the Milners, the Muchas, and Prague. With so many disturbing, unanswered questions bumping around in my mind, it was surely time for me to go there too. And so it was that I went to see Geraldine for that first time. After leaving her to her concert, I met Tom, an old journalist friend, and we went out to dinner at a restaurant called Rudolfino's, in the Old Town near the Charles Bridge. Rudolfino's soon became our favored hangout, for while it stands at the edge of the tourist zone it somehow still belongs to the Czechs, who sit at plain wooden tables in its vaulted basement to smoke and tip back flagons of beer. Unlike most places, it manages to suggest the old times. I have told Tom what I am up to, and that I have tried to tap the secret-police files, the records of the StB. As in most of the Eastern Bloc countries, these files have been at least partly opened in order to take the secrecy out of the secret police, to clear the poisoned air. If I can find the files, I tell Tom, I might discover at last what happened to my family in Prague so long ago. But while I can log into the StB website, I cannot follow the trail, simply because I cannot speak Czech. Tom, who has relocated to Europe from New York for a while, sometimes flies to Prague to catch up with the Czech reporters he has known since teaching at Columbia University's International School. Several of them come to meet us tonight, and we drink wine and slivovitz, local plum brandy. One of the reporters, whose name is Jan, says he can find time to search the files with me, and we quickly make a deal at freelance journalism rates.

The Czech secret-police files are kept at a building on a street called Na Struze in Prague 1, which is in the New Town along the Vlatava River, south of the Charles Bridge and the medieval city. Na Struze No. 3 is stamped with the soul of Stalinism as it stares at a bourgeois neighborhood like a spy from the drab square windows of communism, set into flat grey stucco. The doorstep is dirty, still stained, and you know that beyond it is fear. Around the corner, on the river bank, are the Goethe Institute, standing stolid for old German influence, and the National Theatre, which the private citizens of Prague rebuilt twice after fire, so great was their pride in their city. All around, the buildings are gaudily dressed in the Art Nouveau adapted as a national style in no small part thanks to Mucha's father, Alphonse; but Na Struze No. 3 remains drab and pitiless.

Jan pushes open the heavy street door and walks into the police building with a caution left over from his childhood, into a corridor lined with trash cans divided for recycling. He raps on a small watchman's window set into the wall and is asked to sign a ledger. The old man on duty belches garlic sausage as he speaks and holds a cigarette in his fingers just below a long red sign that reads No Smoking. He insists that coats and bags go into lockers and scrutinizes identification documents; only cards with photographs will do. Then he releases the door to a stairway with the heavy grille of an open elevator shaft rising through the well. Jan takes the stairs.

The reading room for the archives is on the third floor and has long tables set with microfiche readers, the kind of ma-

chines still found alongside computer terminals in the court-
houses of America. The tables have the cheap modern look of
starter-home furniture, as do the chairs set around them, while
the walls are paneled in heavy, mid-fifties wood. Jan says the
room reminds him of Stalin-era classrooms. Old men whisper
to one another and snap photographs of documents with digi-
tal cameras. Jan says these are victims of communism hunting
for vindication, or revenge. He opens a glass-paneled door and
goes into a side office where clerks take requests for files to be
fetched from the archives by name or number, and then hold
them in bins racked on shelves behind their counter. A bitter-
sweet smell of old paper hangs in the air. One of the clerks has
long grey hair, a black turtleneck sweater, and blue jeans. He
could be playing jazz in Greenwich Village in the 1950s. "The
old dissident look," Jan observes drily.

Only a day later he calls me at the hotel on Seifertova Street:
"You're not the only one who wants to know about the Milner
couple. There's a Czech guy called Petr Hrubý who seems to
have been pulling the files. I've looked him up, and he is living
outside Prague. Do you want to find him?" I say I certainly
do, so Jan comes around to the hotel and we call Hrubý. He is
friendly, speaks English, and tells us that he is an old man who
is writing a book on Milner and the Australian spy ring.

The next morning the hotel clerk calls me a taxi with a
driver who has some idea where to find the address Jan has
scrawled on a piece of paper. We drive through the Old Town
and then cross the Vlatava, turning west toward our old neighborhood of Barrandov and farther on to the suburbs. We follow
a road that runs right under the cliffs I remember climbing
atop, and through a narrow valley with the river running on

the left. With new prosperity the Czechs have built a smooth, multi-lane highway, and the cab is a purring new model of the old Czechoslovakian Škoda brand, an everyman's car which smoked its way through communism. The day is crisp and clear and blue, nothing like my memories of the bleak Czech winters. The tramline that had taken us home when we were with Nanny has been extended beyond our stop at the end of the line, I see. I catch a glimpse of the circle where we had stepped down, still with its pub and bakery, and smile at the unexpected recognition. The line now ends at a station called Barrandov Studios, and as we speed by I see the shimmering glass and the bright primary colors of the new Europe. Then we pull off into the past again, through a dim narrow village called Zbraslav, its streets still dirty with snow and grit, its shop windows dark. Above them are squat blocks of uniform apartments declaring totalitarian equality, relieved only partly by the new balconies, bus stops, and playgrounds painted brightly, like the tram station.

Set behind the marching rows of apartment blocks is an airier subdivision of houses with gardens and fences and potting sheds. This is where Petr Hrubý lives. There are cars in some of the driveways and security bars over ground-floor windows. We find the street and the house number, and the taxi driver agrees to wait as I clamber out and walk to a white iron gate to find a bell to ring. At first the place seems abandoned but for a dog that runs around to yap at me. I ring again and double-check the house number, suddenly wondering what it would be like to be summoned to a meeting in a suburban house, only to be trapped by the secret police. After quite a while a small, rounded man appears on the lawn. "Ah! You've come," he says. Hrubý had not heard me at first; his hearing is not what it used to be, and this is the house of a friend, who has lent him a studio around the back. We go back to the studio and sit down, facing each other over a coffee table squeezed into a makeshift living room.

"Since I left Prague when the Communists took over," he says, "I have been teaching college history in Australia." He still has a rich East European accent. "I was lucky. I had my family there. Although my daughter now lives in Maryland, just outside D.C.!" Hrubý makes coffee. "Anyway, I've come back here to visit several times because an Australian newspaper contacted me to ask if I would go to Prague and search for the truth of the VENONA spy ring.

"This was right after the Interior Ministry began opening the StB files. The newspaper came to me because I was a Czech academic, and Czech is my language. There has always been a lot of interest in the spy story in Australia. Let me show you what I found on Milner."

Hrubý hands me a sheaf of twenty-seven pages, stapled together. It is an English translation of a research paper he has written for the Charles University in Prague. He's found a photograph of Ian Milner, he says, but nothing of Margot. Happy to be of help, I rifle through my bag and pull out a copy of the picture I once took of her beside her Mini when she visited my parents' house in Surrey, standing in a summer dress, smiling, with her left hand raised to her throat. Hrubý is pleased and asks if he can use it in his book.

"Yes, of course," I say.

"Now we will go though my paper," he says.

It is headed: Ian Milner—Soviet and Czech Agent on Four Continents (1944–1968) and His Family.

Seven

New Zealand had always been one of those colonies where the settlers took pride in being more British than the British, and one day there, while bent over on the carpet and being thrashed yet again by his father, Ian Milner came to realize that he loathed all that it stood for. He was born in 1911 to a man who owned and ran a boarding school, which was both good luck and bad. Clever enough to soak up his lessons, he became a scholar, ultimately winning the top prize of a Rhodes Scholarship to Oxford. But he was too sensitive to withstand his father, a violent bully who believed that he should spare his son none of the pain he inflicted on his paying pupils. Enduring such a childhood made Milner a match to the profile of the bright young men of the 1930s who would become notorious as spies for the Soviet Union.

As soon as he was able, Milner left home for the local university in Christchurch, where he set about shedding what the secret police files would later describe as his "Christian bourgeois background." His mission in life, he told his friends, was to "break down the class barriers which keep most of us in poverty." Not only did he read his Marx and Lenin diligently, but he moved into a workingman's house. He had an instinctive understanding of the politics of gesture, and his friends soon nicknamed him "Bolshevic." At Oxford from 1934 to 1937 he bonded readily with the generation of young Englishmen trying to comprehend the carnage of the First World War and its unmistakable signal that the confident Victorian world of human progress had died in the trenches. Certainly they could no longer believe that God was an Englishman, and Milner joined the ranks of bright young men who put their faith instead in Marx. He went to Russia with two of his fellows at Moscow's expense, and then wrote for a New Zealand magazine called *Tomorrow*: "What I have seen in the Soviet Union is the most impressive evidence of a successfully working socialist order." He had no opportunity, of course, to explore the gulags or the starving villages of the Ukraine. And back at Oxford, Milner sat through every lecture on literature and politics delivered by fashionable Marxist professors.

His best friend, John Cornford, was a well-known Communist intellectual and among the first to join the International Brigade to fight the fascists in the Spanish Civil War. When Cornford died on the battlefield, Milner wept and wrote a poem in which he promised that "the future belongs to us," and that "we have to prepare for the last battle." There was little that was venal in Ian Milner, but plenty of naiveté. Hrubý shrugs. "It is obvious," he says, "that Milner was one of those innocent Marxist idealists who became a spy and a traitor."

Like Britain's Philby, Burgess, and Maclean, and like America's Rosenbergs, Milner started out sharing views and information with Russians whom he saw as friends in the battle against Hitler's Germany. In 1940 he took a job as a lecturer in political science at the University of Melbourne in Australia and formally joined the Communist Party. That, of course, meant a commitment to "struggle for the revolution" on orders straight from Moscow. Like Anthony Blunt, the Cambridge University professor who recruited the British spy ring, Milner befriended his students and tried to sign them up for the Party. It was also in 1940 that he married a fellow New Zealand Communist whose name was Margaret Leigh Trafford. She was already using Margot for short.

In 1944 Milner went to Australia's capital of Canberra for a job with the Department of External Affairs, the country's equivalent of a diplomatic service. Now able to be truly useful to Moscow, he became a full-blown spy for the KGB—code name: BURR. He reported to Fedor Andeevich Nosov, a KGB agent posing as a Russian TASS news agency correspondent whose code name was TECHNIK. Hrubý's research in the files, I begin to realize, has left no detail unturned.

Milner became the acting director of the Post-Hostilities Division of External Affairs, set up to help plan and then forge Britain's role in a postwar world. Stalin, Churchill, and Franklin Roosevelt were already working on the cartographic carve-up which would lower the Iron Curtain, and so Milner had secured himself an ideal job for the KGB. He even put his old Communist Party buddy Jim Hill on the payroll—*his* KGB code name: TOURIST. With open access to Churchill's secret plans, they helped Stalin stay always a move ahead in the postwar chess game. The Czech StB, no more than a local arm of the KGB, described Milner's efforts

like this: "During his employment at the Ministry of Foreign
Affairs in Australia [it is strange how many of their reports get
some details wrong] between 1944 and 1947 Milner transferred
to us through third party persons valuable materials on political questions."

By 1948 all this had been exposed by the listening operation VENONA. Sir Percy Sillitoe, head of Britain's MI5 spy
catchers, and the up-and-coming Roger Hollis—himself later
suspected of being a Soviet "mole"—flew to Australia to plug
the leak. But this was espionage poker at the top table, and
because the British did not want the Australians to know about
VENONA, they could give them the names but not the evidence. Thus was launched "The Case," which would puzzle
Australia for so many years. That British need for secrecy was
what enabled Milner and his spy ring to escape the consequences. Meanwhile Milner and Margot set off for New York
and a new job at the United Nations Secretariat, where BURR
went back to work. "He kept sending us reports on the activities of individual sections of the UN," reads the StB report,
"and about some leading officials."

In New York the spy catchers of the FBI labored under the
same constraints as the Australians. They had been told that
Milner was a spy but not how he had been identified. "In 2001,
after waiting for a year and a half, I finally got hold of 350 pages
of FBI Milner documents," says Hrubý. "I got them by applying under the Freedom of Information Act. From the moment
Milner arrived in America, the FBI was monitoring his every
move, very carefully. They followed him everywhere. When
he took Margot to Honolulu, they reported that Milner 'was
generally dressed in blue with all blue accessories; wears belted

trench coat, usually hatless, wears beret in stormy weather.'"
We both laugh at the vision of the spy in the blue belted trench
coat failing to notice his tail. "When he took a taxi to Kailua to
go swimming with his wife, they record that too. But despite
all this detail, I was disappointed. This is how they concluded:
'The investigation of Milner until the time of his departure in
1950 failed to reveal that he was engaged in espionage activities
in this country.'" Hrubý unearthed that conclusion in FBI File
65-HQ-58340, Section 3. "I was shocked—I had already seen
the evidence in Prague that he was spying all the time. But then
I found out that there was a reason." The FBI could not set
foot on the United Nations complex on New York's East River
because it was international territory, with diplomatic protec-
tion—which made it a meeting house for spies of all stripes.
"It is impossible to cover his activities there," the FBI report
complains. "However, the New York Office will cover him until he goes to work and after he leaves work." Indeed, the FBI
manpower commitment must have been enormous, which in
itself is a measure of how seriously the Americans took Milner
as a spy.

"Immunity at the United Nations made it so easy for the
Czech and Soviet spies!" says Hrubý, astonished at the scale of
the spy ring he has unearthed. But Milner's time was almost
up, as it happened, for while the FBI agents watching the gates
of the United Nations did not know it, the net cast by VE-
NONA was closing in. The spooks of MI5 and America's National Security Agency were playing a game of cat-and-mouse:
they were watching Milner and the British spies so that they
could follow the trail to the "moles" they knew must be in their
ranks. But the moles managed to stay ahead of the game. While

Milner was busy compiling his KGB reports from UN trips to Cold War trouble spots in Yugoslavia, Palestine, and Korea, someone tipped off his KGB handlers that he had been identified. "The warning could have come from either Kim Philby or William Weisband," says Hrubý. "Both of them were active Soviet agents and had access to the decoded cables sent by the Soviet agents through Canberra to the KGB's Moscow Center."

Hrubý had found a Czech file, number 621743, which reads: "In 1950 we received information from the American counter-espionage agency about a possible repression against Milner working for us as an agent. Therefore, a decision was made to relocate Milner to one of the people's democracies. And so, under the pretext of his wife's medical treatment, Milner took a leave of absence, and left for Czechoslovakia where he soon began working as a lecturer at Prague University." With this information in hand, Hrubý had found the original author of the relocation ruse of Margot "taking the waters," as featured in her obituary. Its writer, John Mansfield Thomson, must have been playing a KGB card forty-five years later, unless Margot had kept up the unlikely cover story of arthritic pianist's hands until the end. The Milners reached Prague in July 1950.

Life for Ian and Margot in the people's democracy was frustrating, even frightening, and they weathered the transition from the ideals of socialism to the terror of Stalin's purges only with difficulty. By 1957 they were divorcing, and Milner was living with a woman he had known in New York, who turns out to have been a spy herself. One of her duties, in fact, was to spy on him. He, meanwhile, kept an eye on Margot and reported back to his StB handlers, who in turn reported on to the KGB. There was a lot more on the Milners, Hrubý said, beyond the Australian spy ring that was now broken. He had become fascinated and worked well beyond his original brief from the Australian newspaper.

And then he reveals that he had found my father's name in the Milner files: "second secretary Lawrence," misspelled with the "w." It is late in the morning now, and we take a break from the small sitting room to stretch our legs around the garden. The dog comes out to yap again, and I check on the taxi, which is still parked out front. The driver has set back his seat and is asleep. The sky is still clear and blue. A woman drives up to the house next door and unloads her groceries.

Hrubý returns to his story: Milner was paid 25,000 *koruna*, Czech crowns, a month for an entire year as a "special assistant" to the StB. This was a fortune at the time; indeed, when the secret police levered him into a job as an English professor at Charles University, the salary was only 7,000 *koruna* a month, and so the StB made up the difference. Milner, then, had earned a comfortable exile, but there was more to his job than teaching English. In the 1950s Prague was used by Moscow as a center for buttering up sympathizers from the West, brought over for "peace" conferences, music festivals, and meetings of such Soviet propaganda organizations as the International Union of Students. In the clash between communism and the West, these were the potential fifth columnists whom Lenin himself had described as "fellow travelers" and even "useful idiots." Milner would be sent to greet and entertain the visitors and spy on them for his masters. This was also the time when a significant group of Communist and left-wing Australians roosted in their Prague "community," writing approving journals of their experiences. Milner informed on them too—indeed, even on some of his former students from Melbourne.

As a Soviet hero, Milner was protected; nevertheless he was expected to pay his dues, and he happened to have defected into a period of Stalinist purges, as Uncle Joe used his last years to cement his new Iron Curtain empire. It was precisely this time when Jiří Mucha and so many others disappeared to serve their sentences in the coal mines. "But many of the targets of the purges happened to be the top Czech and Slovak Communist leaders," says Hrubý, "and Milner was scared. Eleven of them would be hanged in the infamous Rudolf Slánský trial, the show trial of the man who had been the head of the Czech Communist Party and so had run the country. And many others were tortured, shot, or beaten to death." Milner pleaded to return to his old service as BURR at the United Nations. At which point he discovered the reality of his relationship with the StB and its controllers in the KGB. And it was far from benign.

The files put it like this: "Milner underestimates the danger of possible repression against himself. He attempted to visit New York in order to work at the UN secretariat or to return to his fatherland. It is necessary to persuade him by all means that he should not travel to countries of the Anglo-Saxon bloc." Hrubý explains that the original Czech expression for "by all means" is "vsemi prostředky," and it stands for "liquidation." Milner stayed. He was given a new code name, A. JANSKY, and he became secret police Agent No. 9006. He was to teach English at a spy school, the Revolutionary Institute of Linguistics, as well as at Charles University. And then File number

621743 instructs: "In Czechoslovakia Milner can be utilized for work among Anglo-American representatives as well as among other foreigners who either permanently or temporarily happen to be in the country. For contacts use the code name 'Dvorak' and 'greeting from comrade Korin.'"

"Milner was a capable and likable spy," says Hrubý. "Czech colleagues of his at Prague University, whom I know and who are still alive, and a Canadian historian named Gordon Skilling—they were surprised when I told them about his spying on them, and told me they had had no idea. The head of the English Department at the university said to me that they were happy to have him because he was a dependable lecturer and spoke English beautifully." But Hrubý believes that the stress must have taken an increasing toll on Milner. He found files recording Milner's pleas for lighter duties and complaining of bad health. When ordered to accept an invitation to a Christmas reception at the British embassy in 1963, after my own parents had moved on to Cairo, he complied and went, but had a panic attack during the party and fainted. The StB's Captain Hradil ruled that Milner should have three months off, except in "some case of pressing need." He was increasingly left to his academic life, spying on the minutiae of his colleagues' lives but little else, and translating Czech poets into English, for which he was much admired. Milner died in Prague in 1991.

It is not entirely clear, but it appears that Milner's marriage to Margot was rocky by the time they arrived in Prague, because he had already met Jarmila Fruhaufova when they were both working at the United Nations. Born in 1913, Jarmila had gone to America as a student in 1937, before the war. She had married an engineer who had been granted American citizenship, thus gaining citizenship herself. But she divorced Bedrich Fruhauf in 1947 and returned to Prague with a transfer to the city's UN Information Center. Retaining her American citizenship, she came and went, crossing the Iron Curtain well into the 1950s. Jarmila was Milner's mistress for years before he finally divorced Margot in 1957, then he married her and adopted her daughter Linda. But Milner was only one of Jarmila's lovers. I have not found a photograph of her, so I have no idea whether she was a beauty, but she must have had her charms. "She also comes across as an unpleasant woman," says Hrubý. He picks up her story in 1950, when Josef Vins, another of her lovers who was also an agent for the StB, persuaded her to spy on the local UN office. In July that year—the month Milner arrived—she gave Vins the keys to the Information Center so the secret police could copy them and come and go as they pleased, riffling documents, bugging telephones, and changing the tapes on hidden recorders. Stalin's secret police were nothing if not efficient. "After a certain amount of time," says Hrubý, "Jarmila was invited to visit the StB office, politely it seems, and told that it would be faster and more efficient and so a greater help to the cause of socialism if she reported directly to them rather than through her lover Vins. In return, all her expenses would be paid. There was a lot of interest in her because the StB men thought her intelligent, sociable, and a good, useful agent. That is how she is described in the file, anyway. So she agreed to work for them and became Agent HALBICH, No. 7045."

Inevitably her duties included reporting on Milner. In 1953 another informant suggested that she was an American sympathizer at heart, and so they sent yet another man to become her lover and to watch her. By 1956 Jarmila had several lovers, some of them thought to be suspicious while others informed on her. Ultimately, having decided that their "special agent" was "unfortunately not motivated enough" and "unreliable," the StB closed her file and broke off contact. Sexual betrayal was part and parcel of Stalinist terror. Who could have trusted Jarmila? Whom could she have trusted?

Margot, unlike Jarmila, refused to sign up as an agent for her patrons in Prague. Instead she played her own canny game with them. A Communist "fellow traveler" from her late teens, Margot had nonetheless never been a true spy. Certainly she had been happy to organize meetings and spread word of the workers' paradise, but she had never had a code name or sent secret messages to the KGB. Now, finding herself in Prague, she understood the danger and the dread, and she wanted out. She was unhappy from the start, and for all its distortions her obituary in the British newspaper was probably right in asserting that she had wanted Milner to go back to London and talk to his MI5 accusers. That may have meant, however, that Margot wanted him to face the consequences rather than protest an innocence that she must have known to be nonsense. It would have got them out of Prague, at least.

The early StB reports describe Margot as an "external translator and private teacher of English," though there is no detail of when and how quickly she learned to speak Czech. Her file then says: "In favor of winning her over speaks the fact that she entertains contacts with foreigners and with our artistic circles. Against that speaks the fact that she is talkative." The secret police also fretted that, because Milner was having an affair with Jarmila, Margot could be vulnerable to pressure from "foreign agencies." Milner told them that although Margot did not want to lose him, she was thinking of using his adultery to get a divorce, and so to flee the country on her own. Such instability prompted the StB to leave Margot alone. But then in 1952 Margot decided to stay in Prague with Milner after all, even though this was the year that Stalin died, with the Czech purges having reached their most lethal level yet as rival factions fought in the vacuum he had left. First the StB agents checked Margot's mail and called in Milner for another interrogation on his wife's true intentions, and then they invited her to come in for a chat at their "foreign department" at police headquarters on Bartolomějská Street.

Suddenly Hrubý lays the copy of his Milner paper on the coffee table, pushing aside pens and cups. He slumps back, looking tired, gazing out of the window at the cold bare branches of a tree silhouetted against the dimming sky. He has found himself more saddened than surprised by the endless twists and treacheries of his old country as it transformed itself into a nation of spies and informers. He takes a breath, then leans forward over the table as he resumes: "They played good cop with Margot. They told her that they liked to see foreign citizens happy in their country and wanted to help her. She needed a reliable job because she feared being divorced by Milner, and for years she would tell them that she wanted to help them and cooperate but that she could not because she was unwell and that made her unable to work properly. The StB used the word 'lazy' in their reports. They must have known that she was being evasive, and wondered why."

Over the years they found out. Margot proved to be a survivor, and managed to find a niche that brightened her life in Prague. Even as the secret police watched, read her mail, and talked to Milner, she attached herself to Prague's musicians and artists. By the mid-fifties she had made friends with Geraldine—two musical women stranded far from home. Writers are always considered the most dangerous of artists by dictatorships, but the StB made no move to stop Margot making friends with Mucha too, when he was freed from the gulag. Margot was even allowed to travel beyond the Iron Curtain, to London and Australia as an interpreter with Prague's Smetana Quartet, known around the world and now leashed to the Musicians' Union, who were sent abroad to show the world that communism was not so bad. All the while the secret police watched her, and she politely kept them at bay. Or at least partly at bay, because soon life caught up with Margot.

In December 1955 she made contact in London with Milner's brother, who, knowing nothing of VENONA, thought that he could clear Ian's name. He persuaded Margot to come to a room on the sixth floor of the Charing Cross Hotel. A man and a woman were waiting for her. We do not know their names, but we do know that they were from MI5. Margot began by saying: "I have come here to make a strong declaration about the innocence of my husband regarding accusations contained in the Australian Royal Commission report." She demanded to know why the commission members had "made no effort" to contact Milner through the British embassy in Prague, even though they knew that the Milners were in touch with Sir Derwent Kermode, the ambassador there. It was that same cover story from the Margot obituary. I do not know if the agents had their own access to VENONA, but they subjected Margot to the full "debrief." Where had she met Ian? Was he a

member of the Communist Party? How had he got his job at
Melbourne University? At the UN? Margot asked for a drink
of water, and her interrogators urged her to have an alcoholic
drink instead. She was too smart for that, and declined. Had
she and Ian known Russians in Canberra? How did they get to
Prague? At the end of the interview, Milner's brother asked if
there would be "reprisals" against Ian if he returned to Britain.
The answer: "It is entirely possible that he would be arrested
and investigated."

Margot confessed all this to an StB agent named Kublcek
years later, on October 20, 1958, just after I had left Prague and
been taken to catch the train to boarding school. She must have
known that Milner had informed on her, and that there was
no point in denying it. They had been divorced—finally—and
Margot was living on her own, as anxious as ever for a secure
income. Not surprisingly, then, Kublcek started off with his
usual ploy: he could get her a job. Margot answered with *her*
usual ploy: she was ill and could work no more than a few hours
a week. Had she had any "problems" while visiting London? "I
hadn't wanted to at first, but I had a meeting with the British
secret service," she replied. "I worried that lack of cooperation
would confirm the suspicions of our involvement in the Australian spying scandal."

Kublcek set up another chat with Milner to check their stories
against each other. Then he summoned Margot to lunch at a
Prague restaurant. This time she admitted to "several" meetings with the newly created Australian secret service, including one with a man she took to be its chief. After noticing that

her luggage had been searched, she had felt compelled to meet them because Australia was buzzing with rumors that she had been allowed to leave Prague with the Smetana Quartet only in order to spy on its members for the StB. Kublcek reports that he grew more and more suspicious: why had Margot not volunteered this at the first meeting? After lunch, driving her home, he said he wanted to arrange another meeting. For once, Margot lost her nerve, and as Kublcek noted: "Without any context, she started talking about English diplomat Laurence, with whom she is in touch because he is smart, is interested in music, has the same interests—other Englishmen are stupid and uninteresting."

English diplomat Laurence. Afterward Margot demanded a meeting with Milner, now living with Jarmila. They did meet, and Milner then reported straight back to his StB handlers. He told them that Margot had accused him of informing Kublcek of her contact with MI5 and the Australians, and that he had answered that "things have quite changed between us" since their divorce. Fearing that she would be forbidden to travel with the Smetana Quartet, Margot pleaded with him that she was "stressed" and needed assurance that in the future he would say "everything correctly." Her fears were justified, and soon enough her travel privileges were indeed struck down. Realizing that she would no longer be protected as the wife of a valued KGB spy, Margot decided to try once again to bolt for London, applying for an "exit visa" from Czechoslovakia.

It is revealing that when James Hill, Milner's old co-conspirator who had survived MI5's interrogation, heard about the visa application he immediately flew to Prague on a false passport the Czechs had procured for him in Switzerland, so as to travel in secret. The files record that on March 23, 1959, "Comrade Jim Hill, member of the Politburo of the Communist Party of Australia," went to see the minister of the interior, Rudolph Barak, the man in charge of the secret police. "Hill raised a request for us to stop Margot Milner in some nonviolent way from leaving for abroad. If she is to leave for England, we can presume with absolute certainty that she will be used by an intelligence service to unleash a new smear campaign against the USSR and the Australian Communist Party."

Not surprisingly, Margot did *not* get her exit visa. Instead, trapped, she began to cooperate at last with the secret police. "She informs us of her contacts with the British Embassy's defense attaché," Kublcek records, "and about the fact that Mr. Laurence asked her to introduce him to artists and people from the cultural world, finally also of the fact that Laurence invited only Jewish artists on one occasion." Jews who had survived the Holocaust were now suspected of plotting against the Communists, and Margot must have known that this information would entice a secret policeman. It did, and the StB saw their chance to hatch a plot.

Having watched Margot take up with a young, good-looking Czech, the bureau's agents decided the liaison would be an ideal starting point for their plan. Just twenty-six, the young man was happy to spend time with Margot because she taught him English and lent him her car, so long as he washed it after use. After her encounters with Kublcek, Margot agreed to introduce him to the secret police, who, in no small part, "liked him and trusted him because he gave them many reports" on Margot herself.

Jiří Bartoš was an ambitious young fellow who had joined all the right Communist organizations, but it was something else that impressed the secret policemen: "He comes from a bourgeois family, makes friends with people who like Western culture and often visits wine rooms. He seems to be a good type." Captain Borivoj Kalandra soon resolved to recruit him, and Bartoš agreed readily enough when offered far better pay than he made as a laboratory assistant in a chemical factory. So it was that he became Agent No. 10005, code named VIKTOR.

VIKTOR's job was to seduce women at the British embassy whom Margot introduced to him. He would be what the secret police called a "social agent," and his job was to set "honey traps." The files show that Bartoš succeeded first with Laurice Roberts, an embassy clerk. Bartoš also became "a close friend of our collaborator at the British Embassy, Ms Veselá." I wondered if the British had ever known about "Ms Veselá." But the files also say this: "His first assignment is to befriend the first secretary of the British Embassy, Laurence, since he is a good friend of Margot and might be an economic spy." This time they got the job and the name just right, spelled with a "u."

Eight

"D id you know that Margot Milner's husband was a spy?" I ask my father. I am with the kids at his house in the Devon countryside, and as usual it is April, and Easter. We arrived in a steady English rain with the wind blowing from the west, and water is seeping in around the window frames. It is the first time I have noticed how frayed his house has become, how worn down by the weather. He has lived here longer than anywhere since he was born and soon after taken to India's Punjab, where his own father was a clergyman presiding over the local Church of England.

Once, he'd said he did not care for gardening, but he has devoted twenty-three years here to just that, planting trees as if to feel their roots. He has pruned old apple trees into fruitfulness and cut back the raspberries, and he has planted rows of beans, peas, and flowers for the house in the old walled garden, a secret garden of childhood escapes in books. The spring flowers are yellow and blue, and the blossoms have been washed off the trees and are scattered over the grass. The gutters drip while moss lays quiet siege along the walls.

Father is eighty-four, Mother eighty, and their fifty-ninth wedding anniversary is next week. On Easter Day we go out to celebrate at a hotel with a good cook and a private room for us. Father has booked and insists on paying. He is Father and Grandfather, and thus in charge. But at the head of the table he fumbles, spills wine on his suit, and is mortified. Never before have we seen such a thing; we know what it must mean. He refuses help from the waitress, mops at his lap. "Never mind, never mind," he forces himself to say, still in his armor. But behind it he weakens.

Now the sky has cleared, and we have taken cups of tea onto the porch. Father and Mother know that I have been to Prague since I last saw them. "What absolute hell," Mother said when I first told her. As we first pulled into the courtyard at the back of the house, Mother had run from the kitchen door toward us, smiling. Luke had been taking pictures of lambs in the fields on our way in and still held the camera. "Look!" he said. "She's smiling!" He pointed the lens at his Granny and snapped one quickly, almost in focus.

Mother reached us as we clambered from the car, and offered her cheek for pecking. "Here at last!" she said with a laugh, though even now she'd stopped herself from smiling. "I was worried about spoiling the supper." And so the old reveal themselves.

For his part, Father had said nothing about Prague, but he'd added that we would certainly have a chat and look at the papers on Milner. "Interesting," he'd said.

And so we waited until this moment, when we were on our own. "Well, of course I remember that Margot had a husband in Prague, and there was a lot of misery because they were getting divorced. Or perhaps had already been divorced," says Father. "But a spy? I suppose it depends on what you *mean* by a spy. Obviously he had his reasons for being there. He was teaching, wasn't he? We hardly saw him, you know. Saw a great deal of Margot, which is no doubt why you remember her. Margot was rather bitter about the whole thing, really, which I suppose is why he—Ian, was it?—stayed out of the way. Strange chap."

"But while I was in Prague," I say, "I saw a man called Hrubý, who is writing a book about Australian spies who were found out in the same operation that caught Klaus Fuchs and the Rosenbergs, and Burgess and Maclean and Philby. He's been through the old spook files in Prague. Milner was in Prague because he'd been a spy for the Soviets."

It is hard to tell if Father knows all about this or not. My guess is that he is playing me along to find out what I know. That is the habit of a lifetime, and certainly he has no great trust in journalists. On the other hand, perhaps he knows little or nothing about VENONA because it was the biggest secret of all—"need to know" and all that. Father has a leg up on a footstool because the doctor has told him to keep it elevated, which infuriates him as he can no longer do whatever he wants to do.

He walks with a stick now, but tries not to use it when others are around. The problem is that he is still waiting for an operation to replace his worn-out hip. Still, he leans forward all the way to top up his cup from the teapot, and does not ask me to do it for him. I offer him the Australian Frank Cain's paper on VENONA and the royal commission report as well as some of Hrubý's chapter. Father says he'll read them on his way to bed. I tell him that he is quite right to think that I am snooping around Prague.

Over the years we have forged an etiquette. He knows what I have always known about Jiří Mucha and Mother, that Mucha might have been working for the secret police, and how that made so much trouble for the family. Even now, though, we talk *around* the affair, the sex, avoiding it. To do otherwise, I suppose, would demean his manhood.

"What about Margot? What did you make of *her*?" I ask.

"Oh, Margot, poor old thing. She was having a tough time and clearly wasn't happy. But she was a nice girl, you know, always very helpful. Harmless, really. In the end she left Prague and went back to London, got a home-based job with the BBC. I expect you know that."

"In the files, in Hrubý's story, you'll see your name. Do you remember a man called Jiří Bartoš?" My father offers no reaction, so I go on. "Funnily enough, I do, from your parties and so on. Young, I think, and handsome. Margot told the spooks that she was seeing you and let them sign up Bartoš, who was her boyfriend, as an agent, and Bartoš was told to target you.

"They suspected that you were something they called an 'economic spy.' In the files they call Bartoš a 'social agent.' Honey traps and all that."

Father looks at me, sideways because we are sitting side by side facing the garden rather than each other. He is calm and smiling with a twinkle in his eye—a twinkle I rarely saw as a child—which I know is there because I have taken the trouble to check this out, and in his way he approves of that. He is still handsome. You don't know your father is handsome when you are growing up, in the way you might know your mother is beautiful, if that is how she is talked about. I have learned, though, that Father has always been tall-dark-and-handsome, and that when they were undergraduates at Oxford he was the big catch for Mother. Now he has let his hair grow longer, its silver wisping almost raffishly over his ears and collar.

"The thing about being in Prague, in those days," he says, "is that you simply assumed that *anyone* who would talk to you was working for the secret police in one way or another. Otherwise they would not dare to speak to you in the first place, as there was sure to be someone telling the secret police on them too. So that was the working rule.

"You know, the extraordinary thing about Prague and the Czechs is just how efficient they were with their informers. You would think it out of character. You'd expect the *Russians* to have that sort of culture, because Russia has always been a terror state. Never much difference between tsars and Stalin. And then the Germans: the East Germans were notorious for having the worst of the Communist secret police, the Stasi. Teutonic efficiency. But the Czechs? Beastly when you have a culture where everybody is snooping on everyone else and there can be no trust between people and so everything has to be secret. Beastly."

Father chuckles for a brief moment, almost with a kind of pride, the pride of a Cold Warrior who fought the beastliness.

"The Czechs had the second-most-thorough secret police system, in fact—the one with the second-greatest proportion of their population as agents of one sort or another, all spying on one another. At the same time there was really no point in being in Prague if you didn't talk to anyone. So we did the best we could."

"Were you MI6?" I ask now. "Or were you really Foreign Office?"

It is something I have wanted to ask for years. In the real world, of course, there is a very narrow line between diplomat and secret agent, whether MI6 or CIA. The first wants to find things out just like the second, while the second often works from the very same embassy, using diplomatic "cover." They are all in it together. The big difference is that the spook chases other spooks. The guys in the trenches actually picking up secrets in the night might be journalists or traveling businessmen. But there were often people from the Office who would turn out to be "attached" to MI6. You'd look at them a bit differently when you found out, though even then they appeared no different from Father. Perhaps it depended mostly on whose payroll they were on.

Father chuckles. "MI6? Goodness, no! We worked together, certainly, but I was always Foreign Office. The MI6 chap in Prague at the time was the military attaché, which seems rather obvious, but there we are! A colonel. Trying to remember his name. German-sounding." It comes to him after a moment, or rather one of two possible names comes to him. "Whatever you do, don't say that I told you. I'd hate to be thought indiscreet."

The second embassy man that Margot had boasted to the StB officer Kublcek of getting to know, I tell Father, was the military attaché.

Mother suddenly puts her head around the door giving onto the porch. "Shall I take the tray?" she asks. This is a signal that time is nearly up for this private chat with Father. In her way, Mother looks forward to our visits. She likes to charm with stories of this old friend or that, the adventures they have had, and lately to remember those whose obituaries she has read. But she has always found it hard work having "children" around the house, and all the more so with grandchildren. She suspects that they have not been well brought up; they like to watch television and cannot be relied on to enjoy tea with the neighbors. All of my wives have been "dreadful" too, however hard they might try at first. Their skirts are too short, their lips too full. The first day or two are best, before cooking becomes a strain and the headaches start. Mother tries hard to please with schnitzels and cottage pies, things she once cooked as treats on the nights before I left for school. At eighty she has at last let me cook a meal to help, and we have driven into town to buy tuna steaks and new potatoes. But she frets that I will make a fearful mess in her kitchen, and loses her appetite.

Her hair has gone white, but she keeps it neat and set. She has kept her weight down too, and the structure of her face remains well defined. She could pass for ten years younger than she really is, in fact, save for the lines, as neat and sharp as pencil strokes, that have crept around her mouth and eyes. She likes to sit before her old-style kitchen stove, warm by her telephone, with the almost miraculously aging cat. Father used to call my mother Cat, actually, and still does when he is happy.

"It's getting chilly," says Mother. "Will you be coming in?"

Soon, I tell her, before turning back to Father, anxious now because I know that time is running short. "Dad, I want to talk a bit about the Muchas," I say. "You know, when I saw Geraldine, she told me the story about how you got her a passport."

Father lets out a brief staccato laugh. Does he enjoy this talk of old times, or is he simply trying to deal with it? "I do remember that," he says. "But it was nothing very special. We didn't have consuls at the embassies in the Soviet bloc, so they put me in charge of passports. And there was a policy to get passports for British subjects stuck behind the Iron Curtain when we could. You'd never know when they might need them. No need for the Czechs to know, of course. But it wasn't just for Geraldine. There were several of these wives."

"And what about Mucha?" Father is silent. But I decide to press on. "I've always felt there was something about Mucha that has to do with Kate."

"Poor Kate." Father looks away toward the south, toward the graveyard, in fact, where she is buried. "You know, I don't think anyone worked out what went wrong with Kate. Perhaps it had something to do with early puberty. And there has been depression in the family. Kate had a marvelous time in Prague, but maybe there was some strain on her too. In the end, these things are a case of nature *and* circumstances. It is a terrible pity."

I know I should back up now, be gentle. But I can't do that. "I came across a book," I say, "by a well-known American novelist, Philip Roth, who also knew Mucha. Heard of him? The book's called *The Prague Orgy*, and I found it because a character in it is said to be *based* on Mucha. You know—he can come and go through the border as he pleases, and holds orgies in his ornate old palace. Roth has one character saying that they all assume he is a spy, so no one tells him anything, but it hardly matters because his job is just to have sex and to put on orgies where the StB can take photographs and stake their honey traps. Then the character even boasts that the Mucha figure has teenage girls available, and that 'everybody, even schoolchildren, is looking for fun.'"

Still my father's face is impassive. But it is too late to stop. "When I read that, I thought of Kate, and the photos I have of Mucha with his arm draped around her."

My father looks over at me now, as if deciding whether to tell me something. "Odd thing," he says, after a moment or two. "We did have a moment like that, when he turned up to stay at the house in Surrey after we got back from Cairo. You might have been there? In fact I think you were. Kate would have been fifteen, I suppose. We'd finished dinner, and had a *digestif* in the sitting room, and were going up to bed when Mucha took me aside and asked if I would mind if he slept with her. . . ."

"What?" This seems bald beyond my fears. "He asked you that? You can't be serious?"

"Oh, yes. Extraordinary, really!" Father chuckles, as if at the outrageousness of it all.

"Well, what did you say?"

"I said I certainly *would* mind!"

That is all he says, and indeed that seems to have been the extent of his reaction. We are both quiet now. I think of Mucha, coughing in the night in the old farmhouse bedroom next to mine. "If I could hear Jiří coughing," I find myself thinking, "then he couldn't have been in bed with Kate." I am calm, strangely, because I understand that what my father has told me is that somewhere in my memory is truth, not falsehood. *Mucha wanted to bed my sister.* Father and I stare out over the meadow, toward the evening, bonded in silence.

Then he goes on: "Of course we expected Mucha to be informing the police. He must have been, since they had only quite recently let him out of prison. And you know that he had been there for passing information to an American journalist? Why would he risk talking to us, or anyone else, if he didn't have the blessing of the StB? But I don't think he took it very seriously. As for the man, well, he *was* extraordinary. Likable in his way, you know. Though he certainly went after the women.

"And then there's Geraldine. She was quite something too, you know. Not quite the victim you might think, either. There was a photographer living in their house, some chap who had been put in there as a tenant by the police, a tenant they had to accept to keep the place, and who everyone knew was there to snoop. If you see Geraldine again, you might want to ask her about the two-way mirror."

My brother and his wife have come to join us at my father's house, so Prague and all things Mucha are banished from the conversation at table. We talk of other things. But when my parents go up to their bedrooms, I pour my brother and me a glass of cognac and go to the bookshelves to search for that book of paintings I had opened by chance on the piano during one of my parents' parties in Prague. On my first trip back to Prague I had found myself in a gallery of medieval art, standing before a painting that seemed exactly like the one that had horrified me so, and which still did.

I had been walking in the park that follows the steep ridge beside the Hrad, looking for a celebrated café with a view overlooking the city. But the café was shut for the winter, and so I sat on a bench outside to get my breath back. With my eye I followed the twisting line of the Vltava below, and on the far bank I saw a half-ruined building, just on the edge of the ancient Jewish Quarter. It looked as if it must be the oldest building of all in a city of so many old buildings. Spreading out my tourist's map, I soon identified this as St. Agnes, a convent which was indeed Prague's oldest Gothic building. I smiled with self-satisfaction at my traveler's intuition, and then hiked straight back down the hill and over a bridge, all the way to St. Agnes.

The convent was just being turned into a museum of medieval art, and a part of it already housed carved figures and paintings going back seven hundred years. I strolled along, learning that Bohemian Gothic was known for its high level of realism. The collection had a figure of the Madonna and Child with a nipple the size of a wine cork at the infant Jesus' mouth. The artists, I read in my guide, are lost to history, known only as master craftsmen of the cathedrals where they worked.

And then I spotted the painting. Set in a gilded triptych frame, it was not large. *The Master of Rajhrad*, read the placard. *Crucifixion Altarpiece*. I stared at the red pigment thrown across the canvas like blood spatter, the spurt from the ribcage of Christ. By his side were the malefactors, their arms broken yet wrapped around their crosses, and there were the grinning executioners, whacking at the malefactors' knees with cudgels and axes. An angel took flight from the head of one, a devil from the other. I had remembered only the devil. The walls closed in. I stumbled for a door that opened to a cloister, and slumped onto a low stone balustrade. Waiting for my head to clear, I saw that I was in a place of beauty. This cloister, I realized, was at the heart of the convent, and lovely with low vaults and chipped columns. It had been patched in places but not spoiled by restoration. Nor were there relics or altars or art of any kind; it was empty, perfectly empty. The light fell soft, and the air was still. Soon a squat woman hurried up, her feet slapping against the flagstones, and told me the cloister was closed, and that I must leave, immediately.

In my parents' bookshelves at last I find what I am looking for. The books have dry, torn covers but are neatly arranged by school, era, and country, among rows of coffee-table books brought home from my parents' travels. I pull them down, these volumes on Bohemian medieval art, and it is in the third that I find the *Master of Rajhrad*. I have the right painting, sure enough. This time, however, I look at it with a cooler, more appraising eye. I am surprised to find the print in black and white, for that blood had flowed red for me when I first saw it.

Now Benedict comes in from the kitchen, pours more cognac, and we go to another shelf, this one stacked with photo albums. We search for Prague. Benedict is touched to see Nanny again and amused by the small soft version of himself gamboling across the stiffened pages. I am looking for Geraldine, though, seductive in her swimsuit, laughing on the beach.

"I read the papers," Father says just before we leave next morning. "Nothing conclusive, is there?"

Later Mother wrote to me, in one of the blue aerogram letters she has used all my life: "I am amazed that you visited the
Muchas. Friends have met Geraldine when a group they were
in was able to see the Mucha house, and said she was *virulently*
anti-British Embassy. It is well known that most of the British
wives were only there if they agreed to 'spy' for the Czechs.
Geraldine certainly was in that category. You also know that
she had reason to hate my guts."

Nine

———————————

———————————

———————————

Ludvík Arazim is a tough old guy, a secret policeman and a
hunter who boasts he has made five hundred kills. Indeed,
he knows of no one who has made more. At least thirty of these
have been wild boar, the prize of the forest, and his family and
friends would feast on the boar he brought home. Arazim loves
to oil his guns and fill his pouch with ammunition, then leave
grey streets for the woods where the secrets are no longer secrets to a man like him.

In Prague, before he retired, Arazim was as much game-
keeper as hunter. He can track a man or watch a woman, scrib-
bling notes of working hours and shopping trips and sexual
assignations, and he knows precisely how to follow along from
the shadows. When he was a young man he had been trusted
with a job to protect, not to hunt, and to make sure his charge
did not stray. It was a big job, because he reported directly to
the KGB as well as to his own officers of the StB, and he often
went to the Russians for bags filled heavy with cash. These he
would pass on to Ian Milner.

"Milner was hiding from British Intelligence, and my job was to protect him," he says with the clear, measured pace of a prepared statement. "It was a simple job. He had worked in intelligence for the Russians when he had been in America and in Britain, but his situation had become complicated. I don't think he was working in intelligence here, or if he was I did not have anything to do with it. I would make sure his stay in Prague was safe. I gave him a special telephone number where he could contact me and tell me what he needed. We provided for him. I would funnel him money, taking it to him every three months or so. We would meet to discuss how to keep his stay here secret. The KGB was behind it all. And Milner was on very good terms with them, so he must have done something very important."

Jan, the Prague reporter, found Arazim in the StB files, where he is named as a handler in the fat sheaf of reports on Milner. Arazim's own personnel file listed contact information which was still good. He is eighty-two and lives with his third wife in a city called Litoměřice, sixty miles north of Prague. It is three months since I was last in Czechoslovakia, and Jan has climbed the stairs to the reading room at Na Struze No. 3 time and time again on my behalf. He has filed request after request, following names I feed him as well as names he sees in the files as they come up. Jan is persistent and tells me he has become involved in the story in a way he had not at all expected. Like most Czechs, he knows that a curtain has been drawn back since the Velvet Revolution took over the Interior Ministry, the so-called Ministry of Fear. But like most, he has also been content simply to know that the files are there and to leave well enough alone.

By now he has become an expert in the reading room. It takes a while for the man with the ponytail and the woman in the white doctor's coat who works with him to find some of the files we want. Jan makes photocopies from microfiche because the secret police files have been stored that way. Quite a few are missing, and Jan learns that they have been shredded. He also comes across unexpected files, and one of these tells us something new about Margot.

It dates from 1965, when, finally escaping from Prague, she moves to London. "Milner comes often to Czechoslovakia," it reads, "at least yearly for the Spring Music Festival. When here, she again resumes contact with Bartoš and the family of Jiří Mucha, where she stays for a certain time. Mucha and Milner have reached an agreement that they will put each other up when visiting their respective countries. In about 1961 we received an inquiry telling us that in London lives a certain Milner who tries to entice Czechoslovakian employees at our London Embassy to private apartments, and that she maintains contact with a man named Dodson. There is some annoyance at this inquiry on Milner, because there is a man stationed at the Embassy who knows her case. A question was asked whether it is known who Dodson is." I can help them on that. Derek Dodson was an old friend of Father's, whom I had understood to be diplomatic rather than MI5 or 6. You never know. Not only was he MI6, he had been suspected of being the mole before Philby was unmasked.

"A member of the London Embassy, Comrade Koska, can answer this query," the report goes on. "Dodson was a First Secretary at the British Embassy in Prague and was found to be engaged in intelligence activity on our soil. From the overall behavior of Milner, we can conclude that she is an agent of British counter-espionage, particularly because she meets with Dodson in England, makes friends with Czechoslovakian citizens, pretends a relationship with Czechoslovakia, and so acts in a way common for agents of counter-espionage." The officer writing the report concludes that Margot should be watched carefully when she is in Prague. And I am left with the question: Has Margot been a double-agent all along? Did she "turn" in order to be allowed to settle in London? Has she been working for *both* Czechs and the British? Perhaps this is what Father meant when he said he had found "nothing conclusive" in the papers I showed him. It is a good phrase. For the more we sink into the archives—into this Prague of memory—the more it seems that nothing is *ever* conclusive. I go to Litoměřice to find Arazim, then, because I hope he may be able to fill in the missing links—the links between Milner and Margot, between Margot and Bartoš and Mucha, and, above all, between Mucha and my mother. Who did what to whom, and why?

Arazim lives on a street named Lisková, and it is hard to find the number listed for his home because it turns out to be a flat in an apartment block. The block must have been built in the 1960s, after the Stalinist era, because the walls are lighter and the windows bigger, and there are narrow balconies that suggest the confidence to live within public view. The block is a hundred yards long, one unbroken façade, and it would be hard to do anything much without the neighbors knowing. When we finally locate Arazim's flat, it turns out to be on the ground floor, and he seems to have used his status to make home improvements. The balcony is screened with glass for a sunroom, and he has staked a claim to the grass between the window and the sidewalk to plant forsythia shrubs and red roses.

Seeing us, Arazim waves and signals that he is coming out. I have asked him to join us for lunch. It is summer now, and a hot day, so he wears a short-sleeved shirt with checks of pink and black on blue. It is tucked into cargo pants with an elastic waistband, and he carries his things in a fanny pack, which gives him the look of a European tourist. White at the temples, with sensible, steel-rimmed glasses, he is still a powerful man—not tall, particularly, but with a hard head set squarely on a thick neck and the stance of a fighter. Somewhere at the back of his closet, perhaps, still hangs the long leather coat of his profession.

He leads the way down the hill toward Litoměřice's riverside town square with its elegant church spire and sooty Town Hall dome. I imagine that we are heading for an old-style Czech pub with beer in barrels, but at the last minute Arazim changes direction and turns up a steep, narrow side street. He is still generally fit, he explains as we walk on, though he has thrombosis in both legs. Finally he crosses a playground of worn grass to a single-story building painted beige, with a long window at the front. This is his club, he explains—clubs having been important in Communist times because they offered better food, and the people there were Party and thus "approved." His hunting club had been approved too, which is why Arazim never had to give up his guns or hunting.

We order beer and drinking water and a plate of sandwiches which come with pickles. A family is spread around a table set before the long window, and a young man comes in to chat with the girl behind the bar, who is not blonde like many Slavs but has a stack of near-black hair. Leaning forward over the table, Arazim explains to me how he was Milner's guard and minder but has not been the kind of policeman to hatch spy plots.

"Milner was assigned a good house on the edge of Prague," he says, "but I never visited inside the house, and I was never privy to his activities. In fact, I don't think any of my bosses at the StB knew anything about his previous life. The KGB was behind that. But I did know that he was already psychologically ill, unstable, before arriving in Prague. It took time for him to fit in here. And it was part of my job to help him do that. I basically found him a very humble and intelligent person who saw his time in Prague as a time to recover and regain his health."

"Did you know Margot Milner?" I ask.

"No, although I *saw* her. Whenever I met Milner to talk, he would arrive alone. Anyway, I knew from my bosses that there was difficulty between them."

Arazim minded Milner for two years, I learn, until 1954. "That year I was transferred. But I'm confident Milner was not involved in espionage in that time, either for the Russians *or* for Britain and America, who by that time were the enemy."

Europeans who once worked for Nazis or fascists or Communists know of their disgrace today and often want to explain themselves. So it does not surprise me when Arazim seeks a moment to do just that; he is not ashamed, exactly, but seems to want me to know of his redemption.

"I joined the police in 1945," he begins, "before the Communists, and I was a keen Communist then because they had defeated the Germans, sent them out of our country. But even in '48 and '49 I had doubts. I had good relations with the regional director of the Intelligence Service, and he recruited three of us to his branch. But when we were ordered to send five people away to the camps, I intervened. I told the regional director they should not be in jail, which got me in trouble for a while. I had a moral problem with what was happening, and so I was transferred to Prague."

Between 1970 and 1974 Arazim was twice "sacked" from the Communist Party after telling officials that he disagreed with the Soviet invasion of 1968. And finally, in 1974, he was retired, at forty-nine. His file in the StB archive records that Arazim "is a chronic complainer." He had even complained about the grounds of his early retirement, according to his file, though now he seems proud of it.

Arazim says he has no knowledge of Margot being used to set up honey traps. And the deal she made with the secret police to send social agents into the diplomatic world came long after Arazim had been taken off the job. But he does know of Jiří Mucha.

"Within a certain crowd," Arazim explains, "people knew of his lifestyle. But not many. It was allowed because of what we called 'industrial prostitution.'" His face betrays not a flicker of judgment at the idea. "The concept was that young women can be used to influence people. And so Mucha was selected to work in prostitution and to seduce foreigners for information."

Along the road to Litoměřice, which is the old highway from Prague to Berlin, I passed a road sign to Terezín, and I am curious. It is an infamous name, of course, having been used by the Nazis as a transit camp for Jews who would be sent on to the death camps of Auschwitz and Dachau to the north in Poland and Germany. Terezín is also a stop on the railway line to Dresden, which made it convenient for German terror and genocide. But most useful of all, perhaps, was the fact that it had been built in the eighteenth century as a self-enclosed fortress by the Austrians, when it was they who ran this part of Europe. That empire had been as autocratic as any, and just as notorious for its secret policemen.

At first sight, Terezín's high walls—shaped as a series of triangles jutting into the plain for better lines of fire—look almost medieval, while from the air Terezín appears as a series of Stars of David fragmented and rearranged around a rectangle, which is a grid of town streets studded by three small parks. The image of Terezín that has stayed in my mind since I was a boy, learning history, is of musicians allowed to form bands and told to play on a bandstand in the park when the Germans wanted to fool Red Cross inspectors that had been allowed in. They wanted to present Terezín as a decent place where the Jews were protected. The wonder is that they succeeded.

It is still early in the afternoon, and I have time to spare, so I turn east off the highway to follow a country road through fertile fields toward this dark but fabled place. There is wheat and potato and cabbage and green meadowland with black-and-white cows, their udders heavy with afternoon milk. The farms look old-fashioned. There is little traffic, and I cruise, without stopping, right into the heart of the town, where I pull to the curb by one of the parks. In a stroke of the Fellini-esque, a bicycle race is apparently under way, with helmeted riders in bright racing colors buzzing by me in syncopated rhythms.

On the corner of Prazka and Machova, the map in my guidebook shows a Ghetto Museum, and a checkpoint for the bicycle race has been set up on that corner. The riders peddle up, gulping air from the climb over the fortifications. Marshals click stopwatches and note times on clipboards. There are a half dozen fairground stalls too, with striped canopies, offering the contestants water and juice, and for the spectators Pilsner beer. There are not many of those on a weekday afternoon, but the air is festive. I buy myself a coffee.

Racers fit their feet back onto their pedals and swing out around the corner onto Prazka, hunch over their low bars, and sprint into the next leg. Just behind the marshals I see the very bandstand where the musicians must have played for the Red Cross inspectors. The racers and the crowd seem oblivious to this history. Perhaps, even now, that is the idea. I sit on a park bench to read through the Terezín chapter in the guidebook, then find my way through the bicycle race to the entrance of the Ghetto Museum. The building had been used to process the Jews of Prague into the ghetto, and most of them out again. Exhibits chronicle the work gangs sent into the fields to grow food—but there was never enough, so people starved. Wall charts illustrate how the Germans compressed 140,000 into a town where 3,500 had lived comfortably. The old were strewn head to toe in the attics of the building, and died of cold in winter. A glass case holds a puppet figure of a rabbi, made as a rag doll by a girl. And in the grand entrance hall, with its heavy staircase rising up from a polished marble floor, the curators have placed a towering sculpture of cheap suitcases, covered with labels of the names and destinations that signify the transport of Jews to death: Auschwitz, Dachau, Treblinka, Buchenwald.

To the east, down Prazka and over the Ohre River, where the racers have cycled, the Austrians built the *Malá* Pevnost, or "small fortress," in 1780. This handsome structure houses a parade ground as well as a house for the garrison commander and a military prison. Its most famous prisoner, according to my guidebook, was Gavrilo Princip, the Bosnian Serb who assassinated the Austrians' Grand Duke Ferdinand in 1914 and so lit the fuse for the First World War. That is a distinction of sorts. Later, when Hitler's friend Reinhard Heydrich was sent to run Czechoslovakia in the first of the Nazis' many conquests, he turned the *Malá* Pevnost into his SS headquarters and its military prison into the heart of his campaign of Nazi terror.

After Heydrich was assassinated by Czech resistance fighters, the Nazis used Terezín with special ferocity. Historians estimate that 32,000 prisoners passed through the jail and that most of them were Czech rebels, rather than Jews, and that 2,500 died here. The jail block, painted a yellow ochre, is on the left, along the moat just beyond the gate, and it seems terribly small to be the place where all those people were jailed, where all those people died.

Above the entrance the Nazis wrote "Arbeit Macht Frei," Work Brings Freedom, their welcome to the camps. I do not expect this; I have not seen the nametag of slaughter before, except in photographs, and it is shocking. The black painted lettering is still clear, which seems odd to me, but, then, it was not so long ago that they were painted there. There is no guide on duty today, so I am left to wander. I walk past the guardroom to a blockhouse running the length of the north wall and marked Block A. Its three dormitories, with their low, vaulted ceilings, look familiar, like movie sets, with rows of stacked bunks no bigger than coffins, the dark old wood worn smooth to a polish. There are wooden lockers which seem out of place, a mockery, as if offering any right to possessions had been maintained. There are long refectory tables with benches. In one corner is a single lavatory, walled and with a door for a measure of privacy. In the third barrack room is an old cast-iron wood stove for heating. The cracked blue and white tiles around the base picture boats sailing serenely on open water. I try to imagine what a prisoner must have thought, gazing at those tiles.

On the west wall of the courtyard I find a communal bathroom with white enameled sinks, a single iron tub, and showers laid out in a row. Cold white tiles line the walls. The shower stands are made of copper piping left exposed, neatly soldered with wide drencher heads. They would suggest the humane; at least the prisoners might keep clean. But this too is an illusion, for this bathroom, constructed only in 1944 to fool the Red Cross, is every bit as phony as the bandstand of Terezín. I run my hand along the tiles and test a shower faucet. Nothing.

The bathroom gives way to Block B. There is no one else here, and I hear only my own footsteps. Each doorway opens into deeper darkness. My eyes strain to make out anything at all. There are no bunk beds and lavatories here, only cells with thick stone walls and coarse stone floors. They are moist with damp, and the air is heavy, reeking as if unchanged since the last prisoner screamed. These are isolation cells and torture chambers, places of death going back 230 years and yet which might as well be medieval. Iron rings are set in the walls, and narrow, shaftlike windows set up high are blocked with iron grates. Some of the cells have no windows at all, with only the remains of wall lamps in narrow passages to light the way for guards. The walls are filthy, where I can see them at all, and blotched with dark stains. Here, it seems, there has been no attempt to renovate or whitewash or cover up. A framed sign on the wall in the courtyard explains that the last men in these cells were Germans, rounded up by Soviet soldiers and Czechs after May 1945.

I grope along the walls as I go deeper into the block, and I find a cell door open. A single beam of light falls though the window, and suddenly there is a fluttering in the air, and I catch my breath in terror even as I register that the light falls on a restraining ring, a dark spreading stain caught forever just below it. My eyes adjust, and I see a movement behind the crossed iron bars up high at the window. There is a second fluttering through the dark, and I see two small birds settle on the top rung. I stand very still and watch them as they watch me. They are house martins, I see now, and I can make out their tight round nest wedged into one corner of the window shaft. They are nesting like a metaphor, even in this place of so much death.

Ten

———————————

———————————

———————————

The next morning I drive with Jan into the countryside east of Prague to look for Kamil Pixa. Deputy head of counterintelligence after the war, Pixa had kept the job within the State Security Police, the StB, when the Communists took over. Searching for Jiří Mucha, Jan had found his name in the files because it was Pixa who had arrested Mucha and sent him to the gulag in 1951. My last interview, Arazim, had been a secret policeman on the street, but Pixa was scheming at the very top. He has refused to see me.

Jan had telephoned him at his house in Prague, and he listened silently as Jan pitched the idea of his talking to a foreign journalist about Mucha—it was a personal story, he explained. But Pixa said, "No." He was long retired and had no interest in talking about those old times. Jan had found him in Prague easily enough because the StB kept watch on its own men, and we had learned that they rarely left the addresses listed in their files, even after the collapse of communism. But Pixa's file also listed an address for a *chata* out in the country, and as it is now July, we wager that he might well be there.

Pixa was born in 1923, we have learned, and ran afoul of the Stalinist purges soon after jailing Mucha. Yet he somehow survived. Forcibly retired from counterintelligence, he had taken over Propagfilm—producing propaganda and short movies with hidden messages, which meant that he could travel abroad to market them—but he had been reprimanded again when the StB reported him for trying to sell Hollywood movie scripts he had written, and planning to keep the dollars for himself. Little do we know, however, that Pixa has his own story from the torture cells at Terezín.

Passing through industrial suburbs we approach a beaten landscape of collective farms which seem to have failed like the rest of communism. By the time we reach Nymburk there are hedges and copses again, and the low buildings of traditional homesteads. The address we have is Kersko Community No. 172, but this appears nowhere on Jan's map. This is unsurprising to Jan, as "community" will be something like a camp, with plots carved out in the 1950s and given to Party men deemed to have earned their weekend *chatas*: the bigger the man, the bigger his cabin.

We stop at the village pub for directions to a road that takes us two miles to a dirt track on the left. After a half-mile or so, the track dives into a pine forest so thick that the way is paved only with pine needles. It is the sort of place where the wolf might be keeping watch for Little Red Riding Hood, where witches offer candy to lost children. Suddenly Jan turns onto a dusty lane that would be pale brown mud if it were raining. It runs straight, with cottages and cabins laid out on a grid as strict as any industrial city center. The cottages are made of dark wood and seem to be decomposing slowly into their own yards, long ago cleared from the woods to be planted with shrubs and vegetable patches. Overgrown hedges and chain-link fences protect them from searching eyes. Few have numbers visible, and we get lost. Finally Jan finds a club with tennis courts and a restaurant with tables laid out on a terrace, and a covered well where men and women are drawing water into plastic flagons. It is hot, this late morning as we climb from the car, and bugs swarm around us. A waiter comes out, and he fetches the manager, who knows Kamil Pixa and directs us to his house.

A fence around the property is some eight or ten feet high, and the front gate is closed, held with a chain threaded through the links and around the iron bars that form the center posts. I peer through it but cannot make out any house for shrubs run amok. A dog barks. There is no bell of any sort, so we simply call out: "Mr. Pixa! Mr. Pixa!" The dog barks louder. But it is not getting closer. The padlock holding the chain to-gether is open, hanging on its hasp. I can just squeeze my hand through the links where they are cut for the chain, giving the lock enough of a wiggle that it falls to the ground. I unravel the chain and push open the gate. "Are you mad?" Jan asks. But I am perfectly calm. "That dog is leashed," I answer. "Listen."

Pausing a moment, Jan in the end follows, and we step onto a path worn into wheel tracks that runs to the right of the bushes. We can now peek through the leaves at a hunting cabin, built in chalet style, with fretwork trimming a shallow roof and small dark window frames. The dog, a white English bull terrier with a hammer head, is looking straight at us from a run with a kennel set at the back. He has stopped barking. Pixa's front door is open, so I cross a patch of grass and walk up to his doorstep. Inside there is a parlor without much light, and two men are sitting at a wooden table set with coffee mugs and a pile of books. They stare at me, saying nothing, but look neither startled nor particularly surprised.

"Mr. Pixa?" I say in English. With no answer forthcoming, I simply forge ahead. "I love your dog. He's English too!" Again, no response. "An English bull terrier!"

I think they understand me, but Jan steps up and translates. The man on the left is older, and his pale calm eyes have not blinked once since I entered. He wears a drab olive T-shirt, its neckline worn out, and a hunting vest on top. Finally he laughs with a small grunt, and I know this is Pixa. He stands up, and I see the knife and scabbard attached to his belt. He walks to the doorway and shakes hands with me.

We are not exactly invited in, but Pixa steps out, shows us to a wooden picnic table with legs sprouting fungus, and sits down. His companion stays indoors; we do not see him again. I am sorry to intrude, I say, and to arrive unannounced, but I had hoped so much to meet him, and we were unable to find a telephone number for him at his country home. I ask him if he speaks English. Pixa studies me for a moment, likely weighing whether or not to tell me to leave. Then he turns to Jan and says he would prefer to speak in Czech. The sun is high and strong, and there is no shade over the picnic table, but he ignores the heat. His face is tanned to leather, with a long nose and scattered moles. Soft white hair flops over his forehead. He is a strong man, hard worn, with oversized hands and the tip of one little finger missing.

Pixa does not ask us what we want to talk about because he already knows. But first he wants to tell us the story of how he happened to become the man who jailed Mucha. He had come from a good family, he says, and before the war they lived in a fine house in the Castle District. His father had been a Social Democrat delegate to Parliament and chairman of the Civil Service Union, the only trade union to survive the Nazi protectorate. The family was involved in the Czech resistance, harboring partisans and the chairman of the Communist Party while Pixa's mother operated a clandestine radio from the attic. It was a delicate balance, but it worked—that is, until Heydrich was assassinated, and the SS and the Gestapo retaliated.

"Our whole block was searched, every house, every corner. My father was away. The Communist tried to escape when the Gestapo came into our house, jumping from a window and falling three floors. His legs were broken. They captured him, but he held out under interrogation for three days."

The sun grows hotter, and sitting here for even the twenty minutes so far has left me sweating, wishing I had brought a hat. But Pixa is still in 1942, with nine years to go. Perhaps he plans an endurance test that will have me passed out in the sun before he gets to 1951 and Jiří Mucha. I wait for him to draw breath, which gives me a chance to say that I don't want to take his whole day and simply wondered what he could tell me of Mucha. Jan is appalled, because it is a breach of protocol to interrupt an old man. If he wants to talk, let him. Pixa rests his hands on the table before resuming. His eyes look as if the blue has been washed out of them. Jan translates sentence by sentence.

Through the window of a school friend's apartment across the street, Pixa watched the Gestapo flush the Communists and partisans from his house. He saw his mother dragged through the front door to be thrown into a waiting staff car. The Gestapo had not given her time to put on a coat or reach for her handbag. Pixa slid away from the apartment through the rear yard, unnoticed, and walked over the bridge, then through the Old Town and Republic Square to the railway station. He got as far as a town called Strakonice, in southern Bohemia, where he had his hair cut, wondering how he might escape to neutral Switzerland. But he was arrested in a Gestapo sweep the next morning.

"They took me to the cells at Terezín and beat me," he says. "The German officer said that I must have been going to see my father, and that they would beat me until I told them where he was hiding. I told them I did not know. Then they brought my mother into the cell, tied her onto a bench, and in front of me they beat her feet. I watched them beat her feet until they were covered in blood and she could no longer walk. After which they came back to me, beat me again until they broke a bone in the base of my spine."

Finally the Gestapo decided that Pixa must really not know where his father was hiding, and moved him on to Dachau, where he was forced to join a bomb disposal squad made up of fellow Slavs, most of them Czech partisans. "We started an underground at Dachau, and worked at planning an escape. But we were betrayed, and again I was taken for questioning. But now I felt nothing as they beat me because the nerves had gone dead when they broke that bone in my spine. The Gestapo officer crouched and looked at my face as the guard beat me with blow after blow. He simply could not understand why I did not flinch. And then he said: 'This is one tough Slav! Stop, and give him my lunch!' I knew I needed food if I was going to stay alive, and so I took the officer's lunch and ate it eagerly."

Pixa rises stiffly from his bench at the table, and for the first time Jan and I notice the effort he makes to keep his balance. He places a hand in the hollow of his back and shows us the area where he had taken the beating: "Here! One tough Slav!" He is proud, certainly, yet I suspect that he is telling us all of this not so much to make himself a hero as to explain.

After the Red Army liberated the Nazi death camps, Pixa found his way back to Prague, mostly on foot. "I find my father and I hug him. He tells me that the Germans executed my mother. They shot her in the back of the head, in Terezín."

It was chance that led to his new career when he struck up a conversation with an old friend of his father's who had become the head of counterintelligence. Pixa's father resisted, wanting him to go to university, but the friend responded: "We need him. Remember your wife, shot in the head!" And so Pixa brings this preamble to his story to an end: "I became a Nazi hunter, and I took my revenge." Many of those he now caught would meet their fate in Terezín, in the same dark cells as his mother. Pixa is a man who has stood in the eye of the twentieth century.

We have been talking for perhaps two hours, and he goes inside to fetch glasses and water, ushering us to the shade at the side of the chalet. Now at last he will tell me about Jiří Mucha.

"Mucha had been an informant during the war," he says when he returns. "He was working for the general staff of the Czech government-in-exile, which was in London. He was spying on the people around him there, and later when he worked as a propaganda journalist. Mucha came home to Czechoslovakia in the same capacity, spying for the new government as he had for it in exile. Mucha and the American Oatis knew each other like that, because they were both spies. Oatis was the spy we put in jail in 1951 as a warning to the Americans. They were *insulting* us with their spies."

Not knowning the story of William Oatis when I first came back to Prague, I had been surprised when Geraldine described herself as the "wife of a convicted spy," and all the more so when Father told me that Mucha has been jailed for talking to an American journalist. "We used Mucha as a 'blind,'" Pixa explains, "a sort of distraction, because he knew a lot of foreign diplomats and other Westerners who used him as a contact. So we used him ourselves to disseminate false information to them. I ordered him to meet Oatis and to hand him certain information, which trapped Oatis and gave us the opportunity to arrest both of them."

But why? Pixa has just told me that Mucha was working for *him* when he met Oatis. He listens, and answers without hesitation: "I put Mucha away because he was a treacherous bastard, and I wanted to teach him a lesson."

I am stunned. Mucha endured an entire year in solitary confinement, and then three more in the coal and uranium mines of the slave labor camps. *A lesson?* Reading the expression on my face, Pixa raises his voice, his cool eyes glinting. "I will tell you about Mucha," he says. "It is not that he had no morals, but that he did not even know what morals *are*. He was a human monster. I don't think I have ever met a person with less character, less morality, than Mucha.

"He set friends against friends, informing even on the closest. He did this not only for money but for the pleasure of it. He was highly manipulative. He would invite friends over to have sex with Geraldine, which he would watch. Geraldine was his victim, just as everyone was his victim. But she was no saint: Geraldine helped him organize it. Your father is right: they had mirrors, and they used them to watch people having sex. I don't know about photographers. Mucha even offered his wife to me to use for sex. I said no!

"You say your mother had an affair with him? Why not? Mucha had so many lovers that you could not fit them in all the cars of a train. He was a rooster. He cared nothing for these women; he cared for no one. A woman was just another opportunity for pleasure. But there was something in Mucha that attracted women, that made them want to be seduced, to have sex with this man. Maybe his behavior had something to do with a father complex. I do believe Mucha had an extreme father complex because his father was so famous. But it makes no difference: he was such an untrustworthy man that the StB was always suspicious of him. And so we used him but kept a certain distance from him." Pixa struggles to his feet and makes a sweeping movement with his hands. "Let me give you some advice: *never become friends with the Mucha family*."

I reach for the jacket I have laid on a log pile by the door and start to thank him in English while Jan is shaking his hand. But then Pixa gestures for us to sit back down. He smiles, brushes back his thin white forelock, and grins like a fox.

"You know, I met your father once," he says. "I arrested him. He had driven out of Prague on a Saturday afternoon, to the east, to Mladá Boleslav, and he had his secretary in the car with him. He was pretending to be having an affair with her, but we already knew that was no more than cover. We had an informant in your embassy, and we knew the codes too. We had senior people in your secret intelligence service at that time, so it was not so secret to us! Oh, we had lots of fun with your embassy.

"For instance, when the Party forbade people to leave the country, the British would smuggle them out to Vienna. Once a month a diplomat would drive a truck through the border, laden with oil barrels so in times of shortage they would have their own fuel. They would drive through the border with the barrels empty, fill them in Vienna, and then drive back. But we knew perfectly well that they were putting people in the empty barrels. So I set up a roadblock just before the border. When the truck pulled up, the driver gave me his diplomatic papers and explained that he was on the fuel run. I whispered to one of the soldiers I had borrowed to throw some barrels off the truck. You should have heard the people in them crying out as they landed on the ground!

"But your father: he drove until evening when he reached the woods. Then he turned into a lane and stopped at a large square woodpile. He stepped from the car, leaving the engine running, and walked over to the woodpile. He had come to collect a secret letter from the anti-Communist bandits we had at that time. The woodpile was what agents call a 'dead-letter box.' Then as he reached into the woodpile, he was grabbed by three policemen I had hidden there! He pulled back his arm and started to run into the woods while his secretary climbed into the driver's seat and tried to drive away. So we fired our guns to stop them. One bullet caught the lapel of your father's jacket, putting a hole in it, but it did not hurt him. Another, a ricochet, went into the secretary's bottom. As your father surrendered, I told one of the men to steal his papers so he could not prove that he was a diplomat, with immunity from arrest."

Pixa's men took their captives back to Bartolomějská Street, the biggest police station in Prague. "I noticed that the woman was limping. I watched her and saw blood coming through her skirt. But she said nothing; she was silent the whole time—very brave, and beautiful. I sent her to the hospital and they found the bullet there. After they took it out, I had my men take her to the embassy. I locked your father in an office, not a cell, and sat down. 'How dare you insult Her Majesty by arresting me!' he said."

Pixa laughs at the memory: *Her Majesty!* "He was very afraid. But he kept himself under complete control. He had great courage. I kept him there for a few hours while I had his jacket mended so there would be no evidence that we had shot at him. Then I called the ambassador to come get him. I had only wanted to humiliate them. But I also wanted to meet your father. You see, I greatly admired him. You must please greet him for me."

Eleven

On Monday, May 7, 1951, *Time* magazine ran a story under the headline "A Reporter Vanishes." The reporter in question was William Oatis, and he was about to become a far bigger story than anything he'd ever written. *Time* introduced him as a thirty-seven-year-old Associated Press bureau chief who had been sent to Prague the previous summer, after two of his predecessors had been expelled for "unobjective reporting." They described him as a "mild-mannered man who seemed unlikely to offend anyone." He was six feet tall and skinny at 120 pounds. Years later, when he died in 1997, Oatis was remembered as a "quiet and civil man," known for "his dogged persistence in pursuit of facts and his jaunty bow ties." He might have stepped out of the pages of le Carré. Broadcasting into the Soviet empire from Vienna, the Voice of America beatified him as "the first American martyr to press freedom behind the Iron Curtain."

A month before his arrest, *Time* reported, "ominous things began to happen at his bureau." First his Czech translator was "whisked away in a police raid on his home" which took place at dawn. Then two more of his support staff disappeared. Oatis hurried to the American embassy to tell the duty clerk that he was being "shadowed" around the clock by the secret police. He was told to come back the next day; but Oatis never made it. Nobody noticed, apparently, because according to the media record it was three days later when the AP office in Frankfurt, wondering why he hadn't filed a story or answered his telephone, first reported him missing. The American ambassador called the Czech foreign minister and demanded to know what had happened to Oatis, a detail that suggests he may have had an idea of what was afoot. The foreign minister replied that Oatis was under arrest for "activities against the state" and for trying to get "certain secret reports."

The magazine had colorful details: "At midnight, while putting his car in the garage, he had been seized by three plainsclothesmen who stepped out of the shadows." Another version came a bit later. This time Oatis had been rushing back to the shelter of the American embassy when he was suddenly surrounded by cars that forced his own to the curb, then hauled him out and dragged him away. As he himself would later confirm, the secret police cars were Tatras, as they could only have been.

It was Pixa who had urged me to go back to the Oatis file. He wanted me to find an article in *Life* magazine in which Oatis himself had described the interrogation that had persuaded him to confess: "How I Came to Confess," it would be headlined. "I never slapped anybody," Pixa had insisted to me. "I never used violence in an interrogation. What I *would* do is sit the suspect in a chair and then talk to him from behind a desk

I had set up in the interrogation room. I had a typewriter on the desk, and I would type as well as ask questions. Naturally, I would be alone in the room with the prisoner, so I set Mucha and Oatis against each other, telling one that the other had confirmed a fact, and so on. The trick is to make them both believe the other is betraying him, and so it is no longer worth resisting. At no time, though, did I hurt either Mucha or Oatis."

Why, I wondered, was Pixa so keen to be known as the interrogator with the velvet glove?

Oatis spent two years in Prague's old prison at Pankrác, as terrifying as it was lonely. He spent his time writing two hundred songs on bits of scrap paper and later noted, "Didn't sell any of them." First, though, he was subjected to a "show trial." Staged not for justice but rather for political expediency, such trials had been a feature of communism since Lenin and were a kind of theatre of the absurd, the Byzantine truths of which were best expressed by Prague's famous son Franz Kafka in *The Trial.* Oatis's ordeal, staged in the same chamber where the Nazi occupiers had held their trials, and where they sometimes executed their prisoners on the spot, was as Kafkaesque as any, at least as it was reported by the two American diplomats allowed to attend. Oatis had lost his glasses, they noted, and without them he could barely see.

Oatis was particularly dangerous, the prosecutor said, because of his discretion and insistence on accurate, correct, and verified information. In the West such an observation would be a testament to Oatis's journalistic skills, indeed his professional integrity, but the prosecutor did not mean it that way; nor would he have had any sense of the irony in the charge. In a low, flat voice, Oatis read his confession: he admitted taking orders to find out what had happened to the former foreign minister Vladimír Clementis, recently shot. "I am sorry I went in for espionage in this country. I did it only because I listened to the wrong kind of orders from abroad." The American diplomats left out these details they did not want Americans to read, for they too were fighting the Cold War. Oatis's Czech assistants drew sentences of sixteen, eighteen, and twenty years while Oatis was sentenced to ten, whereupon President Eisenhower protested to Joe Stalin and then to the Czechs. Later he imposed trade and travel embargoes on Czechoslovakia.

Only after Stalin died was Oatis released. An American embassy car drove him back through the Iron Curtain to Germany, where he was met at the border post by more than a hundred journalists. One told him, "You're famous now, Bill!" Oatis replied, "I don't see why." The Czechs, he said, had told him that he was being freed in response to a plea for mercy from his wife, Laurabelle, who had married him three months before he went to Prague. Nobody believed this. The newsmen wanted to know if Oatis had been tortured by "the Reds." "No," he replied, "I was not. The treatment varied from time to time, but in general it was good." He balked, however, at questions of why, then, he had confessed, accurately identifying American embassy staffers and other reporters as spies. "That's a pretty personal matter," was all he said, "and I would rather not answer that."

It is strange that there is no mention of Jiří Mucha in the published American record of the Oatis case, nor in Oatis's own descriptions. He wrote a six-part series for the *Washington Evening Star*, complete with dime-novel style illustrations in black and white, and the feature for *Life* magazine as Pixa had remembered, which was reprinted on front pages of newspapers around the world. The "Czech secret police officer" who had befriended Oatis, and "at dinner gave him background information" to "smuggle out through the U.S. diplomatic pouch," is never named, though Oatis for the first time does describe having dinner with a Czech secret agent. Clearly, American intelligence decided not to publish Mucha's identity, for their own reasons.

There was a third version of Oatis's arrest, the first to come from Oatis himself: a Czech who had once applied for a job at the AP bureau came in one morning offering details of where Clementis, the foreign minister, could be found. Oatis turned him down. The Czech forced a photograph of a house into Oatis's hands, and Oatis dropped it into a desk drawer. His visitor fled as six secret policemen burst in, seized the photograph, and cried out "Espionage!" He was taken to Pankrác, where he met his chief interrogator. Oatis says he never knew Pixa's name.

"His eyes were a cool, pale blue behind thick steel-rimmed glasses, and under them the flesh was folded into pouches," wrote Oatis in the *Evening Star*. "His hair was washed-out blond. His face had the pallor of a dead fish. It was twisted into an exaggerated grin. When I asked, 'Who have I been talking to?' he flashed that hideous smile. 'Just call me the Boss,' he said." Pixa confronted Oatis with his own notebooks, which included the notes Oatis had made while having dinner with his friend the Czech secret agent. Pixa told him that the American embassy was doing nothing to help him, a tactic designed to demoralize him. The Boss then suggested that Oatis had also gone to the U.S. military attaché with a report of plans to convert Prague apartment blocks into military quarters. True enough, answered Oatis; he had. It was a story he had heard at the Indian embassy, and he had gone to ask Colonel Atwood, the attaché, if it was true.

"Prisoners make fantastic confessions," Oatis wrote, "because they feel that their only chance to save something out of the wreckage is to do what the police want them to do." In his case, "much of the answer" lay in "a 42-hour interrogation that began at 4 a.m. on the sixth day of my imprisonment." Pixa had told him: "If anyone opposes us, we ruin him. You'll talk: everyone talks here." Guards took turns in keeping Oatis awake while Pixa sat at his typewriter, tapping out ever more detailed and incriminating confessions. "I had been awake for something like 42 hours. They would not let me sleep for 42 hours. They would not let me sleep until I signed, so I signed, because of my absolute helplessness, convinced that my only hope was in playing their game." Clever Pixa.

The CIA must have worried that Pixa had "turned" Oatis and persuaded him to work for the StB, but Pixa made no such claim to me. When Oatis got home, the CIA kept him in a hospital for a while to recover, fearing that he was tubercular. They also took the opportunity to ask him a lot of questions. Counterintelligence calls this "quarantining" and "debriefing." The minutes of the Senate's Church Committee hearings on intelligence record that Oatis was "released into the custody" of the editor of the Associated Press in New York. After a while he went back to work, spending the rest of his career as the AP correspondent at the United Nations.

No journalist could ever claim to know more of what went on in that labyrinth where even the FBI was forbidden from following its suspects, and Oatis's colleagues admired him for unrivaled access and expertise. Not long ago I had dinner in New York with Oatis's son Jonathan, himself a journalist with Reuters, and he was shocked by the idea that his dad really had been a spy and thus an entirely different sort of Cold War hero.

But when he came to think about it, Jonathan remembered his mother saying that Oatis would "never be allowed" to work abroad again. And, of course, he had worked for the Military Intelligence Agency, the forerunner of the National Security Agency, in the Pacific theatre during the war. The family would joke that the clicks and buzzes on their telephone meant that it was bugged. It was fun, when they were kids, that Dad had an obsession with detailed observation. Oatis always liked to count the passenger cars on trains, for instance, working out how many passengers they might be carrying.

I applied through the Freedom of Information Act to see the CIA files on Oatis, and eventually the agency's information and privacy coordinator sent me a thick manila envelope with *Central Intelligence Agency* stamped at the top right corner. Inside were seventy-four documents, all of them described as "previously released records" and none of them particularly revealing. Mostly the sheaf of paper consisted of newspaper reports from the time, though the *Life* magazine article was missing. There was one mysterious American government memo, however, with the sender, recipient, and specific agency all blacked out. The date was left legible—30 June 1953—but the memo number, beginning SC, was obscured. It reads: "Mr. Papich advised today that the FBI has not conducted any investigation concerning Mr. Oatis, and that their files contain no derogatory information about him." I *was* interested to see translations of Czech and Russian reports of the case sent home from the American embassy in Prague, and *Pravda*, the Russian newspaper ironically named for the "Truth," offered details I had not seen before: ". . . in 1944, he attended a special espionage school in Minnesota, in 1945, he studied at the military espionage school in Michigan."

But by far the most interesting thing I found in the CIA dossier was, at last, a single reference to Mucha: his name included in an embassy translation of a Czech radio report from June 1968. It recorded that "five Czech nationals" who had been jailed for "betraying state secrets to William Oatis" had been "rehabilitated," including "the writer Jiří Mucha" among them. It was the time of the Prague Spring, and a judicial commission had reviewed the old case, deciding that the "investigation methods" had been "illegal," that the secrets involved should never really have been considered "state, official or economic secrets," and that, in the final analysis, there really had been no crime.

Mucha had gone to jail with Oatis. Geraldine told me that Jiří "always liked to be at the center of the action," and this time he certainly was. She also said that it was only *after* Mucha came home from the gulag that he had agreed to cooperate with the secret police. Of course it is hard to establish who knew what at any given point, and who might be telling the truth. StB file 2733 comes from Mucha's "personnel" archive, and records: "Mucha was arrested in 1951 and charged with espionage for passing some information to American journalist and spy William Oatis. The information concerned some 10 to 12 Czechoslovak security and military officials rounded up by the police on charges of engaging in activities against the state." This is more like the sort of information a spy would gather, whereas a journalist would write a story on, say, the execution of a foreign minister.

The report goes on: "Mucha was accused of gathering their names, positions, details regarding their activities in security and military circles and the reasons for their arrest, and telling Oatis. Mucha fully collaborated in the investigation, confessing to charges of espionage." He also confessed that Oatis was "using the cover of a foreign journalist for espionage activities in which I personally assisted him." For this record, Pixa had seen no need to mention that he himself had *given* Mucha the information for Oatis. But he could not resist a character assessment: "Mucha is through and through saturated with bourgeois ideology and therefore could have ended up in no other way than as a spy of western imperialists."

Mucha's real slipup had been agreeing to have dinner with Oatis in the first place. He was double-crossed, and that was why he "paid the price in full," as Geraldine likes to say. He performed dutifully enough at his own trial and was sentenced to six years in the labor camps, with a fine of thirty thousand Czechoslovak crowns as additional punishment. Having already spent nearly a year in solitary confinement in Pankrác, he would serve more than two years in the coal mines and later in the uranium mines before being released in 1954. Yet it is only because Pixa's intention had been no more than to "teach him a lesson" that Mucha had escaped the firing squad.

His book *Living and Partly Living* is the diary Mucha kept of his first year in the mines. He took the title from T. S. Eliot's play *Murder in the Cathedral*: "Yet we have gone on living,/

Living and partly living." Mucha scribbled in notebooks by the light of a miner's lamp at the coal face where the fresh coal is hewn, in the same hiding place where he read all the smuggled books that kept him sane. And so the books came in while the notebooks went out, all through the hands of a man named Honza, who was a professional miner, a "civilian" rather than a prisoner. He even managed to smuggle in copies of London's *Daily Telegraph*, the newspaper I would one day work for, and they were a mere four days late. This strikes me as extraordinary: where did Honza get his copies of the *Daily Telegraph*? Certainly they were not on sale at the local newsstand.

Mucha writes in a dry, ironic style the Czechs admire, one that suits their mordant humor. Geraldine has observed that Jiří was fearless, and the book bears this out. The only thing he seems to fear is the loss of beauty and joy in life, and the loss of hope for humanity. In the opening paragraph he is eighteen hundred feet down the mine, sitting on a log covered in coal dust, writing his book in a darkness lit only by his "solitary flickering light." "And in this darkness which has fallen all about me there glows like a lamp the tiny flame of faith in man—flickering, tremulous. The question is: will it survive?"

An old man who had spent five years in a German camp before being locked up again by his own side tells Mucha of the horror of a night spent listening to the restless movement of men facing execution in the morning. Their wooden clogs would bang on the floor above, and all the prisoners would kneel down to pray, which the old man describes as "a beautiful moment."

I read *Living and Partly Living* for a second time, searching for clues to the nature of Jiří Mucha. Careful always to protect his shell, he recalls driving through Czechoslovakia with an American journalist scouting for German invaders in 1939: they have trouble persuading taxi drivers to go as far as the border because the drivers' courage cannot match their own. There is no mention of Oatis. But since much of the diary has Mucha's musing on life, freedom, and the nature of people, there are clues to his own nature.

In solitary confinement Mucha's thoughts turn to his childhood: "It was a rich childhood, surrounded by the beauty of the world." Mucha remembers the green Atlantic rollers off the coast of America, the snowcapped Alps, and the streets of Paris. "I can remember nothing but beauty. No wonder I regard it as the real substance of the world." And then this: "Sometimes it seems to me that I have taken a lot of zigzag roads, that I am apt to rush in headlong where I should hold back, that I act unwisely, and that I have an adventurous or even unstable disposition." He is constantly in search of "the purest note." On page 88 I read: "Freedom is where you act as you think. It is, of course, true that you can always act in accordance with your conscience, albeit at the risk of death. But death is not freedom." He writes of "the urge to live at all costs" and suggests that people "roam about because they have a yearning in their hearts." He wonders if they would stop roaming if they could direct their yearning onto just one person—which suggests that Mucha knew he was incapable of that.

The chapters are named for the months in which Mucha wrote them, and "November" finds him remembering his first wife, Vikta, as they walked through a Paris evening, stopping at a bench in the Luxembourg Gardens. "Her heart was beating as fast as that of a little bird held in one's hand," he writes, in prose worthy of a romance novel. A church clock struck the hour; a bus roared by, the sound of its engine lingering into the distant streets. The lovers whispered their intimacies. But then Vikta seemed to wake from their reverie, and peered into his face. "'Be careful,' she said. 'You may just be in love with love.'"

Mucha makes no comment on this wisdom, and Vikta died of tuberculosis soon after, on the French Riviera, where they had gone in hopes of improving her health. Then the Germans invaded France, and Mucha had just enough time to bury her before running on to Britain.

But it is a passage in "July," the first chapter of *Living and Partly Living*, which stays in my mind: "People are like butterflies. Beautiful as long as you watch them from a remote, aloof point of view. But a butterfly under a magnifying glass is a monster. In close-up its hideousness surpasses all imagination." He goes on to reveal that he has "become fond" of only two people during his first year in the gulag, one a butcher, the other a professional cardsharper. "Clearly," he writes, "morality does not come into it."

Mucha's year ends with his transfer to a second camp. By May he is writing: "I am losing touch with the world I know." There have been escapes, lockdowns, and punishments that took away extra rations and the musical instruments of an ad hoc band. A guard shot himself. A fellow prisoner was trapped in a mining accident, crushed by a rock, and taken to the hospital where he had both an arm and a leg amputated. "This is what people must feel like," he writes, "when they get old and begin to lose their grip on life."

But by "June," Mucha's final chapter, he has been moved with a group of prisoners to a new camp, and they "feel as if an iron gate has opened before us." This camp is also a slave-labor mine, a uranium mine ticking with Geiger counters measuring radiation, but it has whitewashed houses for barracks, lawns and flowerbeds, a "pleasant breeze," and a sky "vaulting over it from horizon to horizon." Mucha wonders: "Is there really something new in the air, or have I ceased to notice the barbed wire?" He has adapted to his environment.

The intelligence officers of the StB who decided to recruit Mucha wrote that he would make a useful spy because he was sophisticated, worldly wise, and had a network of influential friends in the West. They also saw that he "knows how to ingratiate himself and move in any kind of company." He knew "how to get people on his side" and had "an ability to quickly and cleverly respond to his environment." This turned out to be an asset in the camps as well.

As a student he had taken up medicine for a while to please old Alphonse, who wanted his son to be a doctor. It had not lasted, but he had learned enough to persuade the camp commanders that he could be useful as a medic in their clinic. That way he would work half a day in the mines and half in the easier world of the clinic. One of his jobs was to persuade sick prisoners who had learned to be terrified of doctors that it was safe to seek help at the clinic. *Living and Partly Living* ends with an explosion in the mine, after which Mucha tries, but fails, to save a victim punctured with dozens of small wounds. One night, straying too close to the barbed wire, he is shot at by two machine guns; a successful escape, after all, brings down discipline like a dark curtain. Finally he runs out of notebooks for his diary and abandons the project. Two years later, when he is released in 1954, he signs up for service as a collaborator with the secret police and gets a new code name.

From now on, Mucha is ANTY. A secret police file on his recruitment confirms the fact that Pixa had double-crossed him. "Mucha was a recruited agent of the Interior Ministry under the handling of Kamil Pixa. We later found out that much of the information used was devised so he would confess and so help convict Oatis. Mucha made his confession on the understanding that it would not be used against him but just for entrapping Oatis. But it was used and he was sentenced. He is aware that he confessed to something he did not do. Before his arrest he was politically unenlightened on our country. Only afterward while in prison did he study Marx and Lenin, dialectical and historical materialism, and come to grips with happenings in our state, coming over to our side. He is also aware that his release came with our help and that he is to some extent compromised and obligated to us."

Jan and I wondered why Pixa had urged me to find Oatis's article for *Life* magazine; we could not see why it should matter so much to him. Did he want to prove that he had been man enough to renounce the violence he had endured in Terezín? The violence, if not the terror? They were, after all, a part of each other, and had consumed most of Europe. The next time Jan went to the archive at Na Struze No. 3, the man with the grey ponytail told him that he had found another file on Pixa, this one dating from November 1962 and signed by Captain

Stefan Kohl. It was written nine years after Pixa was purged from his job as deputy head of counterintelligence but was still on the books of the StB. The file finds Pixa in trouble again. It does not specify why he is in trouble, only that he is in custody and accused of murder.

It is an old murder, and the report begins: "In accordance with paragraph 164 of the penal code, I am initiating an investigation into a case of suspected murder." It seems absurd—a secret policeman in a Stalinist state being accused of murder: but then the secret policeman lived within smoke and mirrors, just like his victims. "Ferdinand Lotrek was arrested 27 October 1949 and taken to Pankrác prison. On 10 November he was escorted to be interrogated at Ruzyně prison in Prague. There he was interrogated and subjected to brute force by Kamil Pixa, officer of sector 1 MNB, and several of his subordinates. According to the testimony of former Ruzyně prison commander Norbert Kana, his deputy Bedrich Muras and security officer Frantisek Hromek, the interrogators ordered that Lotrek be placed into a dark isolation cell in a straitjacket. Only after several days, when someone noticed a smell emanating from the cell, was Lotrek transferred to the prison hospital in Pankrác in a desolate health condition. He died shortly thereafter."

Pixa got away with it by blaming his subordinates; he claimed that his victim had been beaten beyond recovery *before* he had arrived on the scene. Unfamiliar with the playbook of torture at Ruzyně, he had thought the use of straitjackets was routine. He had avoided the place, having himself been threatened with its terrors under Stalin. This, Pixa explained to Kohl, was because he had made a mistake during the investigation into Rudolf Slánský, the Party boss purged in 1951, subjected to a notorious "show trial" of his own, and executed. And Pixa went on to explain that he had been "a suspect under surveillance" after complaining that "the Slánský case had not been cleanly done." He was saved from the Lotrek murder charge only when Kohl unearthed the autopsy report explaining that Lotrek had died of "natural causes." Clearly, someone had been smart enough to take care of the autopsy report.

This, I realized, was the Prague of Jiří Mucha at the time he met my parents and seduced my mother.

Twelve

Secret police files make for rather unusual portraits, and Europe must be filled with them, waiting like unopened sketchbooks. Here is one of the first I read on Mucha, a report of a party on October 26, 1950, at his house on the Castle Square: "A pornographic film was screened and foreign diplomats had sex with a prominent Czech actress and other women who were present. The foreign diplomats who were present can be identified as Col. Skelton, defense attaché at the British Embassy, Col. Ginder and Major Whitman, both from the U.S. Embassy in Prague, and a diplomat from the Swedish Embassy. Among the Czech women present was actress Dagmar Zikánová." Zikánová! She was not just an actress but a movie star, who would go on to star in *Closely Observed Trains*, a hit movie by Jiří Menzl, which reintroduced Czech cinema to the West in 1966. "Whitman, arriving drunk, immediately approached Zikánová. Whitman is reported as saying that he is certain that his maid is not working for the StB, but he is suspicious that a listening device has been installed in his apartment, and that he is probably under surveillance from a villa next door. Then he turned the conversation to the political situation, and said that it is possible that a war will break out before Christmas. He vowed to get even with everybody then, as he will have a special license for operating in a theatre of war. He also expressed interest in discovering any Americans who are working for Czechoslovakian security organizations. The American movie *All the King's Men* was screened first, and then pornography provided by Mucha.

"While he was speaking to Whitman, our source for this information noticed that Skelton started having sex on the rug with one of the women, while Ginder lay beside her and kissed her. Meanwhile, Whitman went to an adjoining room to have sex with Zikánová, who ran out of the room a short while later, laughing and announcing that Whitman was a bad lover."

There is no clue to the identity of the informant, though since it was in 1950, it might have been Mucha himself, working for Pixa.

I try to imagine my parents at a party like this, but cannot. As the child tucked up in bed and kissed goodnight, I had seen them in my mind sitting at a long polished table with candlesticks, the best china, and countless crystal glasses filled and refilled with wine. The conversation would be dazzling. The notion of Mother disappearing into an adjoining room in her empire-line evening dress would have been unthinkable to me. As, indeed, it is now. Of course the porn movies would have been different from today's, more like those old French postcards with girls in chemises bending over for a bare-bottom spanking from a man with a mustache, animated in creaky black and white.

When I try to imagine Jiří Mucha at his party, that is easier. The secret police recorded that he had parties like this all the time. Just before the event on October 26 they had watched him take pornographic films around to Colonel Skelton's house for a party there. "There was group sex," they wrote in their report, adding that Skelton frequently entertained at home and regarded Mucha as an invaluable "adviser" on "romantic affairs." I can see Mucha back at home in the grand hall of the Castle house, with its gilded mirrors and heavy old commodes, its library shelves and Art Nouveau paintings: he is lounging in a chair, as if on a throne, dribbling smoke toward the ceiling, talking lazily of this or that, half a hooded eye on the flickering screen, an actress's face between his legs as he exercises legendary "potency" at his whim.

That would fit the image of Mucha I have carried in my head all these years. I sat in hotel rooms in Prague for hours reading Mucha's memoir and flipping through the files, running late for dinner. After a while I thought how odd it was that so much of what I learned fit seamlessly with my memories. Those memories are few; I met him perhaps a dozen times when I was eight and nine, and then once more when I was thirteen and he visited my parents' house. At heart what I remember is the slouch, the languor, the curling smoke, the slow eyes and the calm, quiet voice with just enough of an accent to be clearly foreign. And I remember the stories, or rather his way of telling the stories, and the way people listened to them. When I first read *Living and Partly Living* I had been absorbed by the solitary confinement, the mines and labor camps, and the understated way in which he described them.

This time as I read, however, I was drawn to his introspective musings, and I began to recognize myself, or at least the things that people say of me. This seemed strange at first, but there it was: the adventurous or even unstable disposition, the rushing in, taking zigzag roads. The beauty remembered from childhood, the mountains and seas and, at least for me, the deserts too. The art and the books, absorbed as part of everyday life; the faith in aesthetics, taking refuge in beauty.

British boarding schools are essentially philistine institutions, and they leave beauty as the last safe place for the discontented. I once found a letter from the warden to my parents asking them to stop buying me the colored shirts, narrow ties, and sharp shoes of the 1960s as they fueled my conflict with school. Mucha, Geraldine has said, despised his own son Jan for being a fearful, unadventurous "bureaucrat" without response to art—while perhaps it was I who wanted to be like Mucha, even though as a boy I had had no idea of why, or what would have to be put aside to achieve it.

Mucha hears a piano playing in the gulag and writes: "Somewhere in the distance someone is playing the piano. I am listening with bated breath, gratefully, just as I did as a child when I lay down quietly on the big brown bearskin on the floor to listen to my mother playing the piano." A few words later he describes wandering into his father's studio and disappearing in his imagination into the huge canvases of the Slav Epic, Alphonse's grandiose version of Czech national mythology which is admired mainly by the Czechs themselves. The young Mucha recognized the faces of people he knew—Kozler the locksmith, his nanny Manka, and Old Knap with the long beard. And he inspected his own depiction as a boy with a daisy-chain crown, kneeling forever at an ancient court. His mother was the model for the Slav refugee struggling through a wilderness of snow, stalked by wolves. Mucha treasured memories of brushstrokes and colors, images of spectral wolves in the sky and galloping Tartars, and felt that the world of his father's painting was somehow "more real than the one I moved in." Frightening to a boy, it was also as familiar as day-to-day reality. "It made me view the world as a duality," he writes in *Living and Partly Living*.

File number 5630 of November 8, 1954, comes from the StB personnel section and records precisely how Mucha became agent ANTY after his release from the gulag, to be used for Operation West. First the StB officers carefully review a record that begins in 1939, when Mucha was recruited by the remnants of the Czech Republican government, in hiding after the Nazi invasion, to "smuggle espionage material from occupied Czechoslovakia to France." Offering his particular skills, he was responding to the onset of war as a patriot. "The reason for his recruitment," the file observes, "was his connection and access to Britain and France." He had had an "international childhood," after all, following his father from capital to capital, and had studied both "art history and medicine." Mucha had been a willful, individualistic child, expelled from several schools. The StB recruiters did their homework, following his trail as he signed on as a volunteer for the Free Czech army, went on to London, and then traveled to the Middle East as a journalist for the BBC. They even record his work with John Leman's *New Writing* magazine. Immediately after the war, apparently, he went to Egypt and India to make documentaries, a detail I have not seen elsewhere. Under "Political Activities

and Connections" the file records: "Mucha never joined a political party. He knows people in reactionary parties."

And then there is a mysterious paragraph: "When Mucha
went to the Near and Far East he told the Czech authorities
that he would be gone for two months. But he left for a whole
year. He went absent-without-leave from the Czech authorities. Every time there was a telegram, he eluded his contact. To
avoid the repercussions that would ensue, he went to confide
in a friend on the staff who told him to go away and write a
detailed analysis on every country he had visited. He was not
punished." Mucha, the file goes on, "is romantic and adventurous. His interests are in literature and foreign travel. His
company is highly sought after." His friends are "fellow artists," but he never enjoys going to bars and nightclubs. Instead
he prefers to entertain at home and go to other private parties.
"He is a very clever man with perfect English, French and Ital-
ian." To his recruiters, in short, Mucha had everything it takes
to make a useful spy.

Yet the secret police were anxious about his sex life. On the
one hand, it was something they could use for a *social agent*,
and they did. But on the other, they saw clearly enough his desire for women who were *not* on their target list, and that made
them anxious. Moreover they thought his family life dysfunc-
tional. As far back as 1949, when they were planning to seize
Alphonse's villa, they were shocked by what they discovered.
Report 302-557-36 notes: "Mucha's mother and sister live together in the Artist's villa in Prague 19 and they have a bad rep-
utation in the neighborhood. The daughter has physical fights
with the mother, and they have many male visitors, which they
often change. As many as 23 housekeepers have gone through

employment at the Mucha villa, and all were driven to leave by the Mucha widow's rude behavior and her defaults on payments of their wages. During the war, Mrs. Mucha received only Reich Germans, and spoke only German. She answers the door herself when visitors arrive, and speaks a foreign language so the housekeeper cannot understand. This summer the Ministry evicted Mrs. Mucha to Roztoky u Praha and was readying the villa for Chaing Kai-shek's diplomatic office, but due to changes in the political situation in China, the villa remained unoccupied." It is quite a picture.

The secret police go on to complain that when Geraldine went back to England in 1948 for the birth of her son Jan, so that he would have British citizenship, the family continued to claim her rations for the whole year. This was reported to them by one of the disgruntled housekeepers.

Mucha's sister, the files continue, was having an affair with a man "named Pavlovský," and Mucha had a "physical fight" with him. At the time Mucha was hard at work writing at his father's country house at Železná Ruda, where Geraldine would later wait out his imprisonment with her mother-in-law, the widow Maria. Meanwhile Mucha was having an affair with the wife of the Czech violin virtuoso Alex Placek, in addition to bedding the current housekeeper. When the secret police wanted to know why Mucha was wearing a Communist Party lapel pin even though there was no record of his membership in Prague, that housekeeper informed them that he had joined in Železná Ruda. That was loyal of her, noticeable because loyalty is not a trait much portrayed in these files. Finding it increasingly hard to keep track of this family, the StB decided to find a "reliable comrade" to live in rooms in the villa that they would requisition for him.

"He has disorderly marital affairs," a report complains in April 1951, not long before Mucha was double-crossed by Pixa. "He has had a lover for a number of years about which his wife knows, and there are other lovers." For years Marta Kadlečíková, the long-standing lover, was both his personal assistant and his mistress. Many years later, in the 1980s when Geraldine was away, living in London, this same mistress moved in and lived with Mucha.

At about the time my family moved to Prague, a Mucha handler named Lubomír Kaspar filed an assessment of ANTY. "He is lazy in his reports, but is far more productive now that we have given him a tape recorder so that he does not have to spend time writing them. I emphasized to Mucha that he could do a lot more work. ANTY responded that he is willing to do anything in his power and has no reservations about collaboration." Mucha had been allowed to join the Writers' Union after signing up as ANTY, and was given a job as a screenwriter at the Barrandov Studios; I'd wondered whether they were open when we lived at Barrandov, and this report indicates that they were indeed. Geraldine later confirmed it, telling me that Jiří had been allowed the job because Barrandov had been left short of writers by the purges, and indeed she also remembered meeting Kamil Pixa there, and not liking him at all. Interestingly, the Czechs had been purging the Barrandov writers on their side of the Iron Curtain at the same time the Americans had been purging the Hollywood writers on their side after the hearings of the House Un-American Activities Committee.

"I admire his ability to fight against all obstacles to his literary activities," Kaspar wrote, "even though we are not allowing his work to be printed. He is always infinitely reworking his writing to achieve something better, something recognized. In this he is indefatigable. He is driven by his desire to make an impact on cultural society. We must pay special attention to his personal moral life. He has a Bohemian outlook on life and around his personal conduct. His weakness is women. Mucha takes every opportunity for a woman and even his secretary is his longtime lover. In his home there are striptease games and group sexual intercourse. I pointed these things out to him, and said that he should abandon this way of life, and absolve himself of his mistresses, including his secretary, as these are publicly known and cast him in a bad light."

Ultimately Kaspar concludes that, despite Mucha's Bohemian life, "ANTY can be of value to the StB." This is the only reference I have ever seen in Bohemia—historically part of Czechoslovakia—to being *Bohemian* in the sense of wild and unconventional living.

In his novel *The Prague Orgy*, the third in his *Zuckerman Bound* trilogy, Philip Roth sends his character Nathan Zuckerman to Prague in the mid-1970s, the period following the invasion of Soviet tanks that so brutally ended the hopeful days of the Prague Spring. Mucha is loosely yet recognizably cast as Klenek, a film director who has permission to travel abroad because he is good for propaganda, and because, in some kink of the law, a man may go through the Iron Curtain to visit his family if he is divorced. As luck would have it, Klenek is divorced from his wife, cast by Roth as a German baroness.

The story reflects the very lives recorded in the StB files, in which Mucha was allowed to travel abroad partly as a spy for them, and partly because he was separated from Geraldine, who was living in England, where Jan, or John, their son, had been to university. Geraldine insists that they were only *pretending* to separate, for the sake of convenience.

"Here where the literary culture is held hostage," Roth has his Zuckerman muse, "the art of narration flourishes by mouth. In Prague, stories aren't simply stories; it's what they have instead of life. Here they have become their stories, in lieu of being permitted anything else. Storytelling is the form their resistance has taken against the coercion of the powers-that-be." Then an actress takes Zuckerman to bed and says: "'To be fucked is the only freedom left in this country. To fuck and to be fucked is all we have left that they cannot stop.'" This is an accepted truth in the Europe of the great dictatorships, but I am not convinced it really applies to Mucha. After all, he had been fucking any woman he could seduce all his life, even before the Communists took over Prague. It is possible, of course, that he fucked all the more compulsively after they imposed their Stalinist state. Roth doesn't comment on whether all this spying and fucking for freedom corrupts the soul, but I am learning that it corrupted Mucha.

In the course of our research, Jan discovered that more than one hundred operational files of Mucha's work for the secret police had gone missing. He came up with their index numbers, but when he applied for the files the clerks could not locate them. Eventually we were told that they had been shredded. Of course tons of StB files on paper were shredded in the years before the Velvet Revolution, because the Communists knew their time was up and wanted to cover their tracks as best they could. That leaves the question of why they left the files we did find. Perhaps they wanted the Czechs to know all of those who had colluded, so that they might not bear all the blame themselves, even as they did not wish to reveal the details of those betrayals.

We did find a few reports that shone a light on Mucha's shadow life. In 1955, for instance, Mucha was "able to confirm that Comrade Hajšman indeed has an extensive intelligence network." There is no record of Comrade Hajšman's fate. Mucha also managed to "acquire compromising documents of the Yugoslav military attaché Zajsko." There is a report of Mucha being "repeatedly seen" in a white BMW car near an StB agent, and the agents wondered if he was tailing him for the U.S. embassy. A file dated September 10, 1958, at precisely the time he was having the affair with my mother, records: "Mucha is chiefly deployed against British and Canadian diplomats in Prague." The officer goes on to say that he has investigated allegations of Mucha's having been dishonest in his reports, but he has declared them unsubstantiated. Mucha, he believes, is simply being lazy again. "Mucha is further deployed against visiting foreigners from Britain and the United States, mostly journalists and cultural figures. Mucha is sometimes overeager to maintain contact with the StB, so that if 10 days pass without a contact, he goes to great lengths to reestablish it for fear, it would appear, that we have lost confidence in him."

The secret police never trusted Mucha. "I have not made a final opinion as to whether he is an agent of the British," this officer writes. "The interest in him from British diplomats, apparently as an intellectual, has raised justifiable fears in me."

His review concludes: "So far supervision is not such for us to be certain that the collaborator is not doubling. Mucha is an opportunist who tries to convince us that he is fully on our side." Indeed, as soon as he was promised that he would be rewarded with permission to travel abroad, Agent ANTY "immediately" worked much harder and produced better intelligence.

Perhaps the affair with Mother had been just the coup he needed, because by 1963 Mucha had his exit visa and came to London, visiting my family along the way. He reported back to his spymasters and they wrote up a report, file number 563063, on June 14. Mucha had had a meeting with Erich Estorik, a principal dealer in Art Nouveau and decorative art in London whom he had known since the war. "He organized an exhibition of his father's work," says the report. "Among his Czech friends it is discussed openly that during the occupation Mucha was in London and had a very close relationship with SIS. Some say he was an agent of the English service SIS." SIS, of course, being better known as MI6. "What reflected this is that many of his Czech friends avoided him and feared him. But he has maintained good contacts in Britain, and that remains so to this day. Many people in his circle of friends understand his contacts with influential British citizens and that makes Mucha's work valuable to our state bodies."

Who, I have come to wonder, was running whom? Did Mother serve the interests of the StB, or get in the way of MI6? Or did she serve MI6, effectively getting in the way of the StB?

Thirteen

———————————

———————————

———————

Jiří Mucha was assigned to Operation Petr, named for my father, in the early spring of 1958, and I imagine him driving through the streets of Prague to meet the handlers who give him his instructions. They have called him not to a police station, or their own headquarters at Ruzyně, but to an apartment not far away, beyond Sekaninová where Nové Město turns drab. To Western spies this would be known as a "safe house," but its Czech designation translates literally as "conspiracy flat." Such places are scattered around the city so that StB officers can work collaborators like agent ANTY and keep their secrets.

The old men whose stories I have heard, and the wads of files recording their days, have at last created in my mind a narrative, frame by frame, of what happened when Mucha set out to hunt my mother. And of why he did it, and of why she responded as she did. Some of the details take me by surprise—the secret police have been thorough in their notes. Other details have come into focus as I crisscross Prague on foot and by tram, guided by memory, seeking backdrops and links, and I can now draw the lines that connect one old typed-up passage from the StB agents to the next.

Mucha drives his old white BMW over the bridge to the briefing, even though he knows that this deep into Prague's era of communism the car is both glamorous and identifiable. He simply will not live in fear. In a city of shortages it is not hard for him to find a parking space, and he pulls over half a block from a plain grey portal, which, like most of the others, needs a paint job. He sits in the parked car a few minutes before climbing out, for that is the rule. Mucha knows the secret police are watching him, and watching for anyone *else* who might be following, or watching. He looks around casually enough, because it amuses him to spot his tail. He gets out, lighting a cigarette. Others scuttle down Prague's well-watched sidewalks; Mucha strolls up to the building's portal, his smoke mingling with the winter fog.

Inside the conspiracy flat, he pulls off a wool topcoat that once would have been expensive and flops down on a low club chair. Everything is worn and dusty in a way that is no longer even notable in Prague. Net curtains hang above the steam radiators in casements under the windows, filtering what light there is. In my mind, Mucha blows out a mouthful of smoke and smiles broadly at his handlers. In the gulag fewer than four years ago, he remains vulnerable, but he will not project any uncertainty to these men smelling of old cabbage and tobacco. They sit heavily at a table, the junior officer holding a note pad and a pen at the ready. They could arrest him, he knows, these men, but they won't, or at least not today. I imagine them as they all light cigarettes, cupping their hands over their matches in slight annoyance at the fact that it was Mucha who had smoked first.

"Do you know the diplomat Laurence at the British embassy?" Captain Kublcek asks. "He is listed as the first secretary and consul."

"I may have met him. I have been going to receptions at the embassy, you know that. I know the ambassador. But I have no idea if I have met *Laurence*. Perhaps."

"His first name is Peter. He is in his middle thirties. He is here with a wife, Elizabeth, and a family of three children. Two are at school at the lyceé, and one is an infant."

"Don't think I've met an Elizabeth. . . . Not yet."

"Laurence is believed to be an economic spy. This is what we need to discover, and he may also be useful."

Eyelids lowered, Mucha listens without much obvious interest as Captain Kublcek explains that Comrade Milnerova— Margot Milner—has told him about Laurence and has met with him. "You know Milner and Milnerova, of course?"

"Yes, since my release. The Milners were among the first foreign contacts I was authorized to see."

"Milnerova has described Laurence as unusually intelligent and interesting to talk to, and revealed that he is trying to use her to meet other people in Prague who are outside the diplomatic circle. Apparently he wants to meet intellectuals and Czechs in the arts community. Milnerova has also revealed that Laurence held a dinner party at his own home, which is in Barrandov, to which he invited only Jews.

"This has raised suspicions of Laurence's real intentions," says Kublcek. "As you know, there are many Jews still in Prague in business, and it's entirely possible they are plotting against the Party like Slánský and his gang. So we have decided to target Laurence."

Mucha, whose mother came from a half-Jewish family herself, is careful to show no reaction to this. The Czechs are teaching schoolchildren that Communists liberated Jews from the death camps of the Holocaust when they defeated the Nazis, which is true, but they do not tell them that a Czech Jew might yet have good reason to fear those liberating Communists.

"Milnerova has agreed to work against Laurence. Since her divorce from Comrade Milner she is having a sexual liaison with a bourgeois, Jiří Bartoš. Do you know Bartoš?"

"No."

"Milnerova introduced us to Bartoš, and he has agreed to work as a social agent. You will work with them. Bartoš can also ingratiate himself with bourgeois people. Perhaps Mrs. Laurence will want to have sex with him. Milnerova says that she appears to be hunting for a man. Otherwise she will have sex with you, and you will compromise her."

This, then, is Operation Petr. The junior officer logs Mucha's responses with care, as any and all details will be important for the ANTY file. No one, after all, can be fully trusted. Kublcek finishes his brief by telling ANTY that he will coordinate with Milnerova to attend a dinner party and musical evening at her apartment, where he will meet Elizabeth Laurence. She is a fair-skinned woman, about thirty years old. ANTY, Kublcek adds, should find it easy to fuck her. He is smirking. Mucha leaves without looking back. His shoulders drop with the effort of it all.

Margot goes over to the old palace on Castle Square on Friday evening, slipping into the usual Mucha party. It is still early in the evening, and though it is dark, people are just arriving. Mucha is in the kitchen, immediately to the right as you come through the door, and past the old sword he keeps by the threshold. The kitchen is fitted with a greasy gas stove and a bulging refrigerator scrounged from the last days of open markets, but it dates from the days when housekeepers cooked for the bishop upstairs. Mucha sits at a refectory table lined with mismatched wooden kitchen chairs. He prefers to smoke and sip wine, ignoring the dishes of coarse meat and potatoes and cabbage set out before him. There is a tingle in the air, as there always is on these nights. And, of course, between the legs.

Margot sits down next to Mucha and speaks quietly. He raises a hand in warning, palm raised flat over the table; it is well known that Margot talks too much. The Laurences have accepted an invitation to her musical evening the following month, she tells him. She will lay on a buffet supper, which Kublcek has agreed will go on expenses. Mucha raises his hand again, though avoiding the gesture of looking around to see if anyone has heard. They make plans for Mucha to take a turn at the piano at Margo's musical evening and sing an old Bohemian love song as best he can with his low smoky voice. Margot will introduce her new friend from the British embassy. The rest is up to Mucha.

If Elizabeth were an actress, or even just Czech, and Mucha was feeling the blood in him, he would take her by the hand and invite her right into Margot's bedroom. An actress or even just a Czech who knew of him would almost certainly comply. But Mucha's instinct tells him to take his time. It is her involvement he needs, not merely any sexual pleasure she may offer. Operation Petr will have to deliver more than a few frames for a hidden camera. And if Mucha himself is to get anything out of it, he should make friends with this new Elizabeth and her husband too. He can add them to his collection.

She arrives in a long red dress that glows in the cold Prague night, dropping low over her breasts, and she wears a necklace around her neck which, though not long, has been carefully emphasized by her hairdresser. She turns away from the cocktails and the wine but makes a fuss of explaining that what she would really enjoy is a glass of mineral water, without ice, and maybe a twist of lemon. Mucha can see her measuring up the men in the room. Elizabeth wears glasses but without self-deprecation, the costly frames designed to highlight her pale eyes, not hide them. She engages every man who stops to speak with her, never losing track of his name, always fascinated by the point he might choose to make. But it's not long before her eye strays to Mucha, for he is the man at the heart of the room. She is a woman, he calculates, who wants attention more than sex, and so he reminds Margot to wait until the last few bars of his Bohemian song before hurrying her over to meet Jiří Mucha, son of the genius of Art Nouveau.

"Oh, I know his work from Paris, how marvelous!" Elizabeth says minutes later, extending her hand as if it might be kissed, and holding it there so that Mucha can lift his fingers from the keys. Releasing her hand, he turns back to the piano and plays an extra bar, then looks at Elizabeth slightly sideways through heavy lids and smiles around his cigarette. "You should call me George," he says in perfect English.

He next sees her at the house in Barrandov, invited to dinner for a table of twelve, half of them Czech, half of them diplomatic. That way they all get to meet one another and, in a posting like this, to stave off the loneliness too. Elizabeth has a beef roast in from Ostermann Petersen, and Laurence has opened a fresh case of a medium but perfectly acceptable claret. Kate, my sister, has handed around the cocktail snacks. Elizabeth, at the head of the table in her own house, seats Mucha, whom she will call George, on her left, while Geraldine is to the left of Laurence. George charms Elizabeth with a few tales of the gulag but many more of his childhood in Paris and his time in London as they seek common acquaintance. It is a giddy night.

Elizabeth's life in Prague—which has been "a bit sticky" to begin with—soon takes on a new dimension. This is more in keeping with the diplomatic life she has intended. She has kept diaries of all her nights abroad, from picnics by the olive groves of Kalamata to late, late nights in the garden dancing clubs of Athens. She has recorded meeting the Dodsons and the Brewsters, and just how she has dressed to please the ambassador. It has been an exciting life so far, and now there is this marvelous man in Prague who is so terribly interesting.

It is not long before George invites the Laurences to a gathering at the house in Castle Square. "Goodness, what a place!" my mother would exclaim. "Did you *see* all those extraordinary objects? George told me they were all collected by Alphonse because he loved the sort of old things and decorations that would inspire his art. Not great art, of course, but wonderfully decorative."

Laurence has made careful note of who is present and therefore who knows Jiří Mucha, because he has checked at the embassy and been told some of Mucha's record. Ambassadors and military attachés have been enjoying the Mucha salon since the end of the war when Jiří took over from his father, who had died in 1939. Laurence has been advised that Mucha plays the role of "consultant," pandering for those looking for love or simply a change from their wives. Between taking mental notes, he chooses to talk to the locals, which strikes him as useful.

"Goodness me, George and Geraldine do have a Bohemian life," Elizabeth says later, knowing perfectly well all that it suggests. Bohemians in that sense have sprouted in London's Soho, drinking too much in pubs and talking loudly all night of art and poetry, and, when the hangovers are not too bad, pursuing the lives of painters and writers. There is said to be free love between these duffle-coated men with their goatees and their long-tressed, willowy women. Between the men too, sometimes. "But I suppose this is the real Bohemia! Those actresses! What could have been going on in the bedrooms! It is quite intriguing!" Elizabeth has a short laugh that indicates an exclamation mark. She is intrigued, and a little shocked.

The weather becomes quite unexpectedly lovely, and Elizabeth has the idea of organizing a picnic in the countryside. "Do you think George would enjoy that?" She calls him up. He would love to, and helps select the venue. He and Geraldine will bring their son, Jan, who is also John, and the children can get to know each other. It will be good for John to practice his English.

"You must come around for tea some afternoon," Mucha tells his new English friends when he is settled on the picnic rug. "I can show you around the house and all my father's treasures."

"Oh, that would be such fun!" adds Geraldine, who is laughing with her head tilted back.

"I'll bring some Dundee Cake," says Elizabeth.

"That *would* be a treat. It must be years since I've had Dundee Cake."

Mucha looks on as the women talk, knowing perfectly well that Elizabeth would rather be talking to him as she offers him more cheese or a hard-boiled egg dipped in sea salt. On Monday morning Elizabeth promptly orders Dundee Cake from Ostermann's, specifying urgent delivery. And several days later, when Mucha first growls in her ear, away from others, that he would love to see her alone one afternoon, she is flustered.

"That would be lovely and, well—I don't know—I am so flattered," she answers, letting herself brush just delicately against his rough cotton shirt. "But alone? Wouldn't people talk?"

Mucha smiles. "Come after school, with Kate," he says. "All you're doing, then, is bringing your daughter to play with Jan."

Later, but only a little later, as summer stretches the evenings and the season comes for country weekends, he invites her to his *chata*, far away at Jeratin.

"I think Peter will be too busy this weekend!"

"Why don't you come up with me, early? There will be room in the car, and I can point out the landmarks. And bring Kate! She can enjoy a weekend in the countryside and play with John."

At the *chata*, Mucha fries pork chops on the stove in the living room, which is also the kitchen, and burns logs at night against the mountain chill.

Operation Petr goes well at first. Mucha is right about Elizabeth preferring attention to sex, but in a way that makes it easier. She wants to see him every day, if only for a few minutes, and they arrange fleeting assignations at park benches and bridges and cafés. Elizabeth drinks weak tea with lemon because she can't get her genteel blend of Earl Grey. They go to the zoo and walk hand in hand. They stroll through Letenské Park, stretching along the cliff from the Hrad, and laugh at the monumental statue of Stalin gazing out over the city. Sometimes they go on to the outdoor café there and get tea, and settle outdoors under the shade of the birches and horse chestnuts. Sometimes they come across other diplomatic wives, and Elizabeth shows off a little to be with Jiří Mucha, and may even take his arm in a way that suggests friendship rather than desire.

George seems to be enjoying it too, though he complains to Geraldine that this affair is taking too much time. He has his scripts to do at Barrandov and likes time at his desk at home as well to work on books. Geraldine, for her part, worries that he is getting attached; he already has two regular mistresses, and enough is enough. She asks if he is quite sure he is just doing one of his favors for the secret police so that they can live in Castle Square. Mucha says he could do without it and suggests that Geraldine bed Laurence just to keep things on an even keel. They invite them to another party, but Laurence turns Geraldine down while Elizabeth is flustered to be opening her legs when she can hear raucous guests just beyond the door. She really would rather not do that again, she says. Often they go to the cottage at Jiřetín with Kate and Jan—sometimes Geraldine too—and Elizabeth is sure that other wives consider her so lucky to have a place to go to in the country. In her way, Elizabeth is falling in love.

George tells Captain Kublcek that she seems to know very little of her husband's business; he must not tell her much. Laurence works hard, apparently, and is on the fast track at the Foreign Office, so of course he is digging for information whenever he can. Mucha is convinced that he really *is* Foreign Office, not SIS. Nor does Laurence seem to be the jealous type. They all appear to be becoming good friends. And so Mucha keeps working Operation Petr.

One night in the autumn, Laurence comes to sit by Mucha at a reception at another embassy, neutral ground. The guests have been circling on foot, accepting crystal tumblers of whiskey-and-soda or martini cocktails from silver salvers, but chairs have been set up so that they can take a few moments off their feet or hold a more private conversation. Elizabeth has returned to circulate when Laurence takes her place. "I thought you should know that the embassy is taking a great interest in your affair with my wife," Laurence says.

"Well, of course," says Mucha.

"We assume that you are cooperating with the StB," Laurence adds. "But why, we wonder, would they ever be interested? Perhaps you would like to pop in and talk about that?"

Mucha smiles at Laurence but says nothing.

The next morning he leaves his palace home and walks past the Catholic offices next door to the steps that drop steeply through an archway to Radnickze Street. He stops at the café on the turn and steps up to the telephone booth at the back, by the kitchen. Jabbing a *koruna* into the slot, Mucha dials the number he has been given as agent ANTY. A female secretary answers, and ANTY leaves a message demanding an emergency meeting in the safe house. He drives down there at dusk.

He is furious. "You incompetents! You ordered me to compromise this English diplomat, and now it's I who am compromised! Laurence said very clearly that his embassy already knows that his wife has been taken by me, so, then, what use can his embarrassment possibly be to us! How did this even get out! It is because you were stupid enough to choose the wrong woman to seduce! Milnerova put you onto Laurence! And did you ever stop to wonder why? Why she gave *him* to you?"

Mucha has spotted an opportunity. Perhaps if he shows enough anger and fearlessness to these treacherous, brainwashing dogs of the secret police, he will be able to cut back his work for them. Surely he is tarnished now, a risk to the service.

"You should know that Laurence invited me to go his enemy embassy and talk to them, because they are assuming I'm reporting to you. My cover is blown. Look—I've offered my best efforts to the Interior Ministry and to our state, but I will never again be trusted by diplomats. Probably not even by my own *friends*."

Captain Kublcek is duly alarmed. He does not wish to carry the blame for ANTY's exposure on Operation Petr, which he brought in through Milnerova and which has so far pleased his superiors. "It is not my fault, and I don't believe any of my men have compromised you," he says. "Perhaps you may have been too bold in your handling of the Laurence wife."

The two men confer, and now ANTY seems almost the captain's equal. It is best that ANTY continue Operation Petr in order to save face, and simply to wind it down gently. He may stop having sex with the Laurence wife, though he may continue, too, if that is useful to persuade the enemy that ANTY has actually been in love with her. He will continue to see the Laurences at parties in the normal way. But by no means should he go to the embassy for what would surely prove an interrogation.

Mucha gets away with playing down his role as agent ANTY. He still sees the Laurences, as it suits both the British and the Czechs to go on as if nothing much had happened. But he has convinced Kublcek that his cover as the social agent is blown, and that all he can do now for the StB is collaborate as an informer. Mucha does not mind keeping the secret police up to date on who is sleeping with whom, and who is up to what. If anything, he thinks of this as a triumph, because he has manipulated this unsuccessful end to Operation Petr into a way of putting a little space between himself and the StB while hanging on to his palace and all his privileges.

Sensing the possibilities, Mucha decides to play a new game with the Communists. He will wind down his role as informer to the police who inhabit the shadows of the streets, and go for the bigger men in the corridors of power. Mucha has known some of them all his life, for they too were born in high places and made their own compromises with the Communists. It is time to persuade them that he can serve his country best if they let him go back to his international life. He tells them he believes that by selling his father's work, beloved in the decadent West, he can earn American dollars and British pounds for Prague's starved coffers of hard currency.

It takes time to get this deal together, but Mucha has learned patience. The officers handling agent ANTY grow frustrated. He is called to a safe house and told that he is "failing to live up to his possibilities." Mucha listens gravely without giving much away.

"Your information is increasingly superficial! You have been of little use to the state! Why should we bother letting you continue in your immoral life?"

Mucha lets his accusers blow off steam before responding. "Have you no memory?" he says, finally. "It was the stupidity of the security police that spoiled my operations against enemy diplomats! I *told* you then that I would no longer be trusted by friends or foreigners. How can I get good information?"

"And what of your visits to the embassy parties? You go to just as many as you did before. We certainly don't believe you are working for us there. You are pursuing your own commercial interests, aren't you? You think we don't know what you do there? You are trying to enrich yourself by selling your father's art!"

"Fools!" Mucha replies, allowing his voice to rise only a little. "I am engaged in an operation that is not for your ears! Go and ask your superiors at the Interior Ministry if you feel so courageous!"

In 1963 his scheme comes to fruition, and Mucha travels to London to make contact at last with lost friends and to meet with Eric Estrovich, who will sell the Mucha art in Britain and America. At the same time the StB files a report saying that agent ANTY, having been found unreliable, has stood down. His new operation goes well, and he is getting just what he wants. Mucha originals sell for tens of thousands of dollars in affluent America. The posters go into print and sell cheaply but as never before. They become part of the wallpaper of Swinging London and the flighty, early days of the drug culture. Mucha comes and goes across the Iron Curtain almost at will, his visas stamped in Switzerland. Before long he is among the richest men in Prague. By 1966 he is allowed to open a foreign credit account in a currency the Communists called *tuzec koruna*, which means that he can buy foreign luxuries and even cars. It is a privilege granted only to senior Party men, Czech diplomats, and the filmmakers and musicians allowed to work abroad. Mucha opens his account with a deposit from Estrovich the art dealer. Before long his account reaches 34,390 *tuzec koruna*, which is 340,390 common *koruna*, and that gives him the local spending power of a Western millionaire.

The British suspect that Mucha is an StB courier, using the art sales as a cover. They log his car coming off the channel ferries into Dover or Ramsgate, and follow his London rounds. From the passenger deck he watches the bow of the ferry plow through the swells of the channel, and pulls up his collar against the spray. He loves to watch the White Cliffs of Dover rise from the horizon, standing for the Britain that stopped Hitler's march and for his own good war. Mucha is welcomed by the veterans of the Prague embassy, because that way the British can at least try to work out what he is up to. But there are difficult moments for Mucha. In February 1968 he is stopped at the English docks and hustled off to meet two men from MI5. They have a lot of questions for him, and warn Mucha that if he fails to cooperate they will make sure that he never again sets foot on Western soil. They know all about his Swiss visas and can stop them with a single call. "Tell us about the time you seduced the first secretary's wife," they ask, and: "We want all the details of your links to the Interior Ministry and the StB."

At least this is the story he tells the StB. Mucha drives to Hamburg on his way home to Prague, and then, according to the secret police report, decides to take the route through Berlin, which in 1968 is marooned in Communist East Germany and split by the Berlin Wall, because it is the most direct.

When he gets back to Prague, Mucha meets with his StB handlers, and this time they refer to him in their report as "former collaborator ANTY." Yet he hardly seems to have retired from the secret service as he tells them of his close call in England. Then he describes his trip to Berlin and how he took the opportunity to stay the night with Elizabeth Laurence. Her husband is now serving in Berlin as the political officer for the British diplomatic mission, but he is away in Heidelberg, learning German, which may or may not be a coincidence.

Mucha explains all of this to Major Joseph Hampl, the officer he reports to now. How, for instance, he had noticed that the straightest road to Prague went through Berlin, and so he had decided to telephone the Laurences to ask them if he might visit. Mrs. Laurence invited him to spend the night before he drove on to Prague the following day. He ended up staying for two nights.

"Mrs. Laurence told me that a mutual friend of ours, Christopher Mallaby, was in Berlin," Mucha tells Major Hampl, "and that when she had mentioned I was coming to stay, he said he wanted to get together. I had met Mallaby in London and also at the Dodsons."

Mucha need not add that the StB long ago identified Derek Dodson as an MI6 agent, though in 1968 Mucha can have no way of knowing that Mallaby will climb the career ladder all the way to the top, to head the Foreign Office. He describes

Mallaby to Hampl as tall and blond, very smart and inquisitive. Mallaby's wife is French, and he has spent several years at the embassy in Moscow. Mallaby hurried over for lunch, Mucha tells Hampl, even though he had a meeting at 2 p.m.

And then agent ANTY tells Hampl what happened to Operation Petr. He speaks softly, as usual, raising an eyebrow from time to time, or giving a quick, self-deprecating laugh. And this, according to the files, is what he says: "The family situation of the Laurences is roughly that neither of them is rich. Laurence worked his way up from very basic conditions as a very gifted student, winning scholarships, which is how he became a diplomat. His wife naturally has a great interest in his career and in that way is loyal to him. She tries to help him, understands what he needs for his work, and is as interested as he is in making the most of his career.

"As for their personal relationship, it is perfectly clear to Laurence that his wife is philandering, but he makes nothing of it because, believe me, she gets on his nerves and, if anything, he is glad to have someone else keeping her engaged. She's constantly in and out of affairs within the diplomatic circle, but most of these affairs would seem to be one-sided. She convinces herself that the man she's in love with loves her too, and that it's only because of good manners and the need to be discreet that he holds back from seeking a closer relationship with her. Where in fact the opposite is true. Every man who gets to know her quickly learns that to have a physical relationship is to court her hysteria and unbearable neediness.

"When I compromised them, the Laurences got together as the tightest team and with complete ruthlessness, I must say, acted to protect their interests. They did everything they could

184 / Charles Laurence

for the best result for their service and government. Laurence is a former officer who has huge self-discipline—not at all the sort of person who can be swayed by any pressure. She, on the other hand, just has a hysterical fit, tells him all about it and then does exactly what he tells her to do."

Mucha will have nothing to do with the suggestion that he should embark on a second affair with Elizabeth Laurence.

Fourteen

Before slipping up with Operation Petr, Mucha had triumphed as a social agent in a much grander operation. Two years earlier, in the summer of 1956, he had been sent as ANTY to London to spy on the Czech exiles he had known during the war, and to reconnect with his more prominent friends. Back in Prague from London, on June 22 he went straight to a safe house to meet a Lieutenant Colonel Balvin for his debriefing, and Balvin concluded that he had made "one of the most valuable contacts to the upper reaches of English society that could be established."

Not only had agent ANTY managed the remarkable feat of sleeping with the former mistress of the British prime minister, Sir Anthony Eden, but she was so in love that she was begging him for trysts anywhere in Europe. Pauline Grant was a celebrity in her own right—a ballet dancer and choreographer—but also a woman who knew *everyone*. The renewal of that affair was hailed as a major coup for the IS–SNB, the foreign intelligence arm of the secret police.

When the StB first sprang Mucha from the gulag in 1954 and turned him into agent ANTY, they had had a good idea of the extent of his social network and how useful it might be. They sat him down in an interrogation chamber and ordered him to list every contact he had ever made, anyone and everyone with social status that he had ever known. They understood what it meant that he had been born into the *haute bourgeoisie*, and they clearly appreciated his talent for making friends and for using them at his will. During the Nazi protectorate he had escaped to the West and used his status to engineer himself a fine life in London. He had operated hand-in-hand with the Czech government-in-exile, which became the postwar government, and which the Party had, in turn, overthrown in their February Revolution of 1948. At the time they arrested Mucha he had been working for Czech intelligence, and it is suspected that he had also been an agent of the British SIS/MI6 since his time in London. Mucha turns out to have had friends and connections beyond the credence of the average man.

There is a transcript of this interrogation, and it begins with Mucha's life as a teenager before the war. His maternal uncle, Zdeněk Chytil, who started the newspaper *Lidove Noviny*, put young Jiří under the wing of his diplomatic correspondent, Hubert Ripka. Together they launched his career with an assignment to Italy, where he reported while also studying art for his first university degree. During this time Mucha managed to become friends with Bruno and Vittorio Mussolini, the sons of the fascist dictator, no less. Chytil was later murdered by the Nazis at Terezín. And as war broke out, Ripka became foreign minister in the Czech government-in-exile in England.

After reaching London, Mucha later told his interrogators, he was levered into his BBC job by Ripka and by Jan Masaryk, who would go on to become the postwar Czech foreign minister, and who would die falling out of a window during the Communist coup of 1948. Whether Masaryk committed suicide remains to this day a great national mystery; throwing political opponents out of windows is known as "defenestration" and is, after all, a great Czech tradition. Mucha, then, seems to have spent nothing less than a lifetime lounging at the heart of history.

Mucha's interrogators asked whether he had known British intelligence agents: he listed four, from Cairo to Warsaw, but claimed that he never "knowingly" worked for them or gave them information. He was then told to list all his contacts in Prague since the end of the occupation in 1945; he came up with sixty-eight Czechs, who included five counts, three of them living "illegally" in Switzerland, Rome, or England. He also knew the owner of the AERO factory requisitioned by the Communists, a film director, journalists, writers, painters, musicians, a former Scout leader who had escaped to South America, and a professor in exile at the University of Dundee in Scotland. Not a few of his contacts are listed in the file as "in prison."

Then Mucha went on to list his British friends, a familiar roll call of the artists and writers who went on to be influential or famous, but at the top are Admiral Lord Boyd of the Royal Navy; Lord Cholmondely, the senior royal chamberlain; and Elizabeth Montague-Scott-Douglas, "niece of Queen Elizabeth." He knew Hollywood royalty too: Vivien Leigh, the star who played Scarlett O'Hara in *Gone with the Wind*, among them.

Colonel Balvin told Mucha to describe his marriage to Geraldine. "I have a good relationship with my wife, but our marriage has not been working out very well for a long while now," he replied. "For several years I have had a closer relationship to Vlasta Plocková, who is much closer to me than my wife. Indeed, I have been trying lately to decide just how to resolve this situation, since Plocková is married to Josef Plocek the musician and is the mother of two children, while I myself have a six-year-old son. It's a difficult problem for me, as I value my wife as a good friend who is always ready to support me. But I am certainly not prepared to sever my ties to Plocková. Plocek recently found out about our relationship, and I suppose if he were to agree to a divorce I would probably divorce my wife and marry Plocková."

Mucha's frank answers seemed to satisfy Balvin and his comrades, and inspired the spies of the IS-SNB to send him on his new mission to England. He traveled now under the cover of a film critic, covering the Cannes film festival.

"During his stay abroad," Balvin wrote, "he adhered to one key aim: to reestablish his contacts from eight years ago. In order to do that, he had to be alert, so as not to arouse suspicion; and, where there *was* suspicion, to dispel it. He would, of course, be one of the very few Czechs his old friends knew who was allowed to travel abroad, but Cannes seemed a perfectly plausible rationale for his trip. His cover was to specify that he had applied for a passport a year in advance, and only through the personal influence of the director general was it approved in the end. Mucha was to present himself as a supporter of the regime, but could admit to a number of flaws if such an admission could be useful to his cover or his intelligence gathering."

In London Mucha looked up his old Hungarian friend Arthur Koestler, best known for his novel *Darkness at Noon* and once a Trotskyite Communist acting as a personal secretary to Stalin, though by now a British citizen. Whose side, Mucha's handlers were determined to know, was he on now? Mucha concluded that he was fiercely anti-Soviet, working for the Western propaganda agency. He went to tea on June 5 with the Czech orchestra conductor Rafael Kubelík, whom the Communists wanted home from exile. Mucha found the celebrated conductor unwell and impoverished, eager to return, but only if he could travel freely on a Czech passport, and only if the Communists punished those officials who had purged the musical community, "righting all the wrongs they committed." He also demanded to be able to choose where he would live. Mucha claimed that he had argued to Kubelík that such reforms were already under way.

But as an intelligence asset, none of Mucha's old friends could match Pauline Grant, and she was without question the coup of his career as a spy. Grant would have been a star dancer and choreographer on the London stage when Mucha first met her during the war. Later, in the 1960s, she would also make a splash as choreographer for that iconic movie of Swinging London, *The Amorous Adventures of Moll Flanders*, based on the bawdy seventeenth-century novel by Henry Fielding, which broke any number of taboos of the cinema at the time. It was as the former mistress and continuing friend of Sir Anthony Eden, however, that she most impressed the Czechs. 1956 was the year of the bungled British and French attempt to seize the Suez Canal from rebellious Egypt—the operation that was widely seen to have brought the British Empire to its symbolic end—and Eden was prime minister. Later made Lord Avon, Eden had also been foreign minister during Britain's moment of shame with the Munich Agreement, which had appeased Hitler by ceding him Czechoslovakia's Sudetenland, and later under Churchill during the war. Reconnecting with his star conquest as agent ANTY, Mucha must have been in top form and was soon talking to Grant with his head on her pillow.

"I met Pauline Grant during the war when we were both working in the theatre," he told Balvin. "At that time she left Foreign Minister Eden for me, but we split up later because I refused to marry her after the war. We met again on Saturday, June 2, at the house of a friend. Pauline, he told me, was very interested in what had happened to me while I was serving my prison sentence, and that she had even got hold of my dossier from the British embassy in Prague." The file, Grant told him, suggested that he had been arrested as a "cover-up maneuver" over his role in the Oatis affair, indicating that the British had suspected him of working for the StB all along.

"On that same evening," Mucha boasted, "I managed to get our relationship back almost to the same level where we had left off before, and in the days that followed, it developed only further."

But, the file records him explaining to Balvin, Grant was much more than a successful artist—she had "contacts in the highest places." She mixed with the leading diplomats and the most senior politicians. Even her husband would have been an unbeatable target for a spy in the Cold War age of nuclear standoff: he was a former RAF pilot engaged in "top secret work on guided missiles."

"For Grant and her circle, nothing is impossible," said Mucha. "She has invited me to a party for some very senior people at the end of July, and insists that she can send a helicopter to pick me up in the evening so I can go to the party, and then spend the night, and it will bring me back to Prague in the morning. She wants to organize an assignation with me anywhere in Europe, suggesting Switzerland in July or August." I can just imagine Mucha drawing on his cigarette, nonchalantly.

Balvin was delighted. "Through her," he wrote, "it is possible to influence even very important decisions. ANTY has a very close relationship with the above named, and she is under his influence. She is willing to meet at any location."

Fifteen

Father was an Englishman who could reveal himself more easily when talking of someone else. For instance, he mentioned, in writing a note for family posterity, that his mother had lost an infant child before she drove her car into a lamppost and died, her chest crushed against the steering column. "She may have blacked out because she was rather depressed at the time." He was eleven and in the front passenger seat, with his sister and younger brother and aunt in the rear. "One must carry on, I suppose," he said when I asked him about it.

Father carried on by winning a scholarship to Radley and then another to Christ Church at Oxford. He stayed with his aunt during the holidays, because his own father, the Anglican priest, had returned to India's Punjab, where he would remain until Independence, after the war. The scholarship to Radley made of my father—who, after all, had come from a reasonably modest background—an officer and a gentleman. Late in life he would sometimes utter things that amazed me: "Radley—ghastly place. Loathed it myself." Which might have prompted me to ask, then, why he had given his sons the same experience—something I never got around to. But on that last Easter visit I did wonder out loud why Grandfather had not seen more of him even after coming Home. Grandfather traveled once to London to meet Mother, who would remember how handsome he was, with his vivid blue eyes, then again to marry them in Kensington. And he had come once more to see the birth of his first grandchild, Kate. The parish he had been granted for retirement was not terribly far from London, but "I presume he had his duties to perform," Father explained.

It turns out that Father had not been the British diplomat caught by Kamil Pixa with his hand in the dead-letter box. But he might as well have been. On the drive back from Pixa's *chata* to Prague I had been elated to hear Father so admired by his enemy, a Communist secret policeman. But then I thought about the dates—which, if Pixa had been purged from his job as deputy head of counterintelligence after Stalin died in 1953, would not have fit. Pixa had also described the guerrillas leaving the clandestine note as bandits who had collaborated with the Germans in the war. These would have been the Benderovce of Slovakia, and when I checked I found that they had been long gone by 1957, mostly to their graves. These doubts prompted me to make a second trip to Pixa. "I knew you would be back," he said.

He went over the story again. There were more details: the secretary had been petite and had dirty-blonde hair. But he could not remember her name. They had caught the "bandit" who had left the message; he was "a fool" and came to "a bad end." I asked Pixa how the StB had known the embassy codes for the message that he had read to set his trap. He laughed:

"You cannot expect me to tell you that." But when he thought back hard he said: "This must have been around 1950 because I was dismissed at the time of Stalin's death. But I am still sure I met your father, as I see this man in you. Perhaps I met him later, with Mucha, when he worked at the Barrandov studios. You must still give him my greetings!" It must have been an earlier first secretary, then, who was caught at the dead-letter box, just as Father had been caught counting tanks. There was a certain type back then, and they were recognized.

I wanted to tell Father about Pixa and his greeting, but when I saw him next it was for the last time. He had been fading at Easter, but now the end was coming fast. Outside his window the Devon trees and hedgerows were only just turning, but he himself had already passed to deep midwinter. He had fought his decline, hiding it valiantly and trying his damnedest to put it to the back of his mind, which is how he had learned to deal with hardship. Lunch dates with old friends were kept because they were already on the calendar. But Father seemed to have no strength to recover from the surgery that had fitted him with a new hip. And his temper was growing short. By July he admitted he could no longer complete the crossword in the *Daily Telegraph*. His mind could follow the clues well enough, but he could not read the words. He struggled over even the headline news with a magnifying glass. Mother bought a contemporary sofa that looked out of place among all the antiques, because she knew he was uncomfortable and hoped he might settle in to watch television—something he had never had much time for—with what was left of his middle vision. All of this I learned from Mother's letters and telephone calls.

Soon Father was down to half-hearing from a single ear, but he would fit the hearing aid and chat as if he could hear the conversation. Admitting that the summer growth had defeated him, he hired gardeners, but the only one who was "any bloody good" had quit when his wife had had a baby and he needed more time at home. "Well," Father said, "we'll just have to let it go a bit." He's dying, I thought. And he was. His hair was getting long, but he could not get out to the barber. Soon his right arm went numb.

Hospitals were places to be avoided at all costs, but after some persuasion Father agreed to struggle into the car for a visit to the optician. "Sir Peter appears to have had a stroke," the optician told Mother. "I'm afraid he must see his doctor as soon as possible." Mother called me shortly afterward: "Charles? It looks like Daddy's had a stroke! Oh dear! We're going to the doctor and there'll be tests. We'll have to be brave." Father had to wait a couple of weeks before going to the hospital for his MRI. It showed a scar of damaged brain tissue, and the doctors said he must have had a stroke after his surgery, always a risk for a man of his age. They needed to take a second look with a higher resolution, however, as their MRI machine was faulty, and they were waiting to have it fixed.

Mother called again to relay the test results. Imagining herself looking after him, she spoke about how they might have to move to another house. Certainly they would not be able to maintain the garden. "It's so terribly sad," she said, "but he is eighty-four." I said that maybe she should have a cry, but she said she didn't want to. She was going to be brave and think of Father and how she could look after him as he had always looked after her. She was worried, though, because they would need help at home, and that would be terribly expensive. Their savings would not last long. . . . But when the hospital mended its MRI machine the doctors discovered that Father had not had a stroke at all. Rather, he had a large tumor growing at the back of his brain, and it was knocking out his systems, one by one. Mother called again, and this time she did cry a little over the telephone.

There was no more planning to move to a smaller house with a smaller garden. Father came home to wait for an appointment with a doctor specializing in cancers of the brain. The surgeon decided that he could not operate: the tumor had spread too far, and Father was simply too old. I wrote my father a letter telling him I loved him, and thanking him for being my father. I asked him to tell my brother Benedict that he loved him and that he was proud of him, because I knew how much that would mean to Benedict, and how difficult it was for Father to say any such thing. I know that he did just as I'd asked, because Benedict later telephoned to say that he had been to see Father and found him a completely different man.

"How?"

"He was sentimental in a way I have never seen. . . . We actually hugged, and he told me he loved me."

Later I asked Mother whether Father had also said he was proud of my brother for what he had achieved in life, even if that wasn't much by their standards, and she said he had not.

"We're just not that sort of family," she explained.

One morning Father came down to breakfast in the kitchen and discovered that he could no longer swallow, indeed could hardly speak. It was as if he were suffocating. Mother said she would call an ambulance, but Father managed to say "no" and went out of the room. Mother called the ambulance anyway, and when she had done that she saw that he was not on the sofa or on his bed. She found him instead in his study, mumbling in fury because he couldn't find the file he kept with his financial statements, and because he couldn't find the key to the shotgun rack. They took him to the hospital. Mother telephoned me in New York and said that perhaps the time had come to fly over and visit my father.

I call an old colleague at the *Daily Telegraph* who is their chief obituary writer, a man with a big voice and old-fashioned suits who still understands the war generation and the stories they like to read. I tell him that my father is dying and how much I would appreciate a good send-off.

"Sorry to hear that," says David. "Tell me about him."

I do, starting with the version of his wartime exploits that had made the front cover of a schoolboy's comic magazine called *The Victor*. A print of it might make a novel illustration.

"Splendid!" says David. "Send it over."

Then we go to work assembling the details of Father's life. "Just the sort of chap our readers love. It'll make their day." The headline on *The Victor* story is "According to Plan," which is very rare in war. David uses the story as the lead for his obituary: "In the first frame Lieutenant Laurence of the 11th Battalion, Kings Royal Rifle Corps, was shown wondering whether the enemy were occupying a lone house, known as 'The Apostle,' near Ponte in December 1943. In broad daylight he and a Corporal Angus crept up close, to find themselves under fire from a hole in the wall. 'You spray the windows while I pop a visiting card through the hole,' Laurence was shown saying as he threw in a grenade and Angus fired his Tommy gun up at the first floor window."

"Having developed such a sure technique," he continued, "Laurence went on to use it again." After two more successful raids on German occupied buildings, Father was awarded the Military Cross, Britain's second-highest award for valor after the Victoria Cross. "This officer has shown outstanding qualities of leadership," the citation reads.

Father is sitting quietly in an upright, cushioned chair when I reach him at the old brick community hospital in Torrington, which is the nearest town to his village. A tray-table on wheels has been drawn up over his lap. He props his right arm, which he can no longer move, on one end, and a glass of water sits on the other. He can still use his left arm and can lift the glass, but his legs have now gone too. The chair is beside the bed, and there is just room for a chest where he can keep a clean shirt and a spare battery for his hearing aid. Father has been brought here from the emergency hospital because it is closer to his house and can provide him a room of his own. His middle vision is holding, and he can see the sun dappling the privet green outside the window. Mother has bought a cot to place in the sitting room because she cannot help him up the stairs, but it will not be needed. I bend down to kiss my father's cheek, which I have never done before and yet seems strangely natural. A nurse brings him tea, and a cup for me as well. He is now struggling to speak, his brain linking the wrong words to his thoughts. At one point he asks for a clean *afternoon*, which makes no sense, and then shows the nurse what he means by pulling furiously at his *shirt*. He seems angry at the ebbing of his power, his life. I ask him whether he feels at peace. "You mean accepting death?" he replies. "Grace? Nonsense, if you ask me."

He is anxious to know if I and my family are safe and provided for. Am I getting work? Do I have a pension coming? How are the children? Luke is sixteen and driving, which is scary. "The risks of life," he says. And is Charlotte, my daughter, coping at last? Well, she still runs up debts and needs money all the time. She is twenty-four. "If I were you I wouldn't give her any more," he says, "and that way she might learn."

"You know, it's hard," I reply. "I still feel I have to protect her as best I can." We have had this conversation before.

"Protect her; I suppose so. Oh well. Life is never easy, really. It's terribly sad, everything that happened. I'm afraid I've made a bit of a hash of things. So. Never mind," says Father.

Some visitors tire him. Jeremy, the vicar of St. Michael of All Angels, who will bury him, calls in, as he does every day. He wears socks with sandals, even with his cassock on as he tosses the incense burner on its chain and leads the chants, and has a host of children in an old stone rectory. He offers comfort and communion at any time, though I wonder if my father is still holding on to his faith. I have my doubts. A woman from a hospice that Father has helped and guided for years as it cares for the dying comes to say that they will serve any need he has, and with love. He looks out the window and says, "I know I won't be seeing home again." It is the only time I ever see him shed a tear. Mother comes, and he grasps her hand, so pleased to see her—weak, finally, with need. When it is time for us to go, he holds on tighter and tells her urgently that he loves her.

Mother and I drive the twenty miles to the supermarket in nearby Barnstaple, a bigger town, to stock up on the better sort of ready meals that she can pop in her oven to save cooking, now that she will be alone. We talk as we have always done when driving together to run errands, and she even laughs a little as we remember her zooming through Berlin in her white MG to buy wine and cheese tax-free at the French commissary, and then on to the British NAAFI for gin and whiskey, and cheap cigarettes for me. This time I have the wheel. As we pass through the Devon countryside she recalls the names of the friends who live or have lived down these lanes that have come to be so familiar in the course of Father's long retirement. Some have been terribly kind after hearing of his illness. Others died long ago, or more recently, and Mother chuckles as she says they had fallen to the habit of skipping first to the obituaries every day to find out whom they should scratch from the address book. "Do you remember the Fayres? They retired to Devon and we went to lunch. For years, you know, I had the *biggest* feud with him!" She chuckles again with a touch of self-deprecation, her head bowed just a fraction, as if in disgrace, but not really, and I can see how even now the old boys find her charming. "In Athens he did the most dreadful thing—the most unforgivable thing to do in Athens! He stole our nanny! And they were impossible to find there! Mind you, she only accepted because it was such hard work dealing with *you*. Kate was always so easy, but you were a devil." We fall silent. "Oh Charles," she says finally. "How am I going to cope without Daddy? I just can't imagine him not being here."

Back at the house, which will really no longer be Father's, we unload the groceries, and Mother goes to the greenhouse at the far side of the courtyard to feed old Oliver, her cat. She calls him, and they purr together as she pulls open the can and fills the water bowl. Then she crosses to the front door to the letter box and gathers in the mail. There is a great deal of mail because a lot of friends have written to say how sorry they are to hear about Father. She sits at the kitchen table by the warm stove and carefully opens each one. "Oh how kind!" she says from time to time. She will have to answer each one, for this is what she has done all her life. Her desk is already piled high with Christmas cards. She always starts on them at this time of year because it takes forever, and she ticks them off against the list she keeps of people who have sent cards last year. The first to go to the post office are to friends abroad, to make sure they get there in good time. Every year, of course, the list gets a little shorter, and it's well below three hundred now. All the marvelous people they have known. . . . "But imagine the postage these days! Phew! I'll have to cut back."

I go to the rack at the back of the pantry behind the kitchen and select a claret to open at dinner. I look at the labels of some of Father's better chateaux but take a table wine, because I know that is what he would do. Nothing these last few years has earned a smile from him like bringing him a bottle of something fine, especially from a vintner he has known in person. But no one is celebrating tonight. Mother warns that there will be telephone calls, which can be a bit tedious. She is having trouble with Father's family, who insist on visiting even though Mother is sure that Father wants no more visitors. What's more, they want to stay with her, to which she has had to say no. They can bloody well find their own bed-and-break-fast. And Aunt Mary is going to bring her husband, though he means absolutely nothing to them.

Soon Mother drifts into conversation about who will get what when she has to pack up the house after Father dies. To start with, what is she going to do with all these *books?* Would I like to take some of the rugs they had gathered when they were in Turkey? And what about the wardrobe I had left in the guest cottage years ago, when I moved to America? Should I take that back? She is sorry, but there is not much silver now, because they lost a lot in the burglary.

Old ladies do this at the end. Perhaps they are becoming focused on the next generations, or perhaps it offers a sort of power. I don't much like it, in any case, and suggest that there is really very little I should take because my own homes get smaller with travel and time. Father had relished the idea of leaving his sword to his grandson because we had joked about knights and dragons when Luke was young. And I'd like some of the family photographs one day, perhaps an heirloom or two from China. "The *sword?*" she says. "I'm afraid Benedict took that the other weekend! I had no idea Daddy had promised it to Luke!" Benedict and his wife Liz live in South Wales, not too far away, and have drawn close with holiday gatherings and in-creasingly frequent visits to lend helping hands. "Liz has been wonderful," Mother says. "Such a help. Benedict has been so lucky. A wonderful girl." And the compliment prompts an-other thought: "I'm afraid I'm going to leave my jewelry to Liz. In my will, though, I *have* asked Liz to select a few pieces for Charlotte, which seemed to be the best solution. I could hardly leave it to Charlotte, could I?"

She goes to bed early. It has been a long day, and she is warm and cozy up in her bedroom. Mother has not had time to prepare the cottage and instead puts me in Father's room across the landing. The house has two bedrooms upstairs in the main building, each with its own bathroom and dressing room, and when Father retired my parents decided they should have their own rooms. There has never been a reason for me to come up here, and as I drop my bag on the floor and look around, I realize I have never been in this room. The window looks over the front garden and across the valley, where on a sunny morning shafts of light divide the mist that gathers among his trees in the meadow. Beyond is the churchyard where he will be buried beside my sister. Father has a heavy wood wardrobe, and I pull open the door. Inside he has a few old Jermyn Street suits and two tweed jackets and a blue blazer and two or three pairs of twill trousers he seems to have worn all my life. Ties hang on the back of the door. I notice the two pairs of jeans he began to wear in the garden a few years ago and a pair of moleskins, for the dirty jobs, that lie crumpled on the closet floor, no longer worthy of a hanger. Shirts are folded into a drawer below. A second dresser holds more shirts, underwear, and a couple of woolen sweaters. Father never did want much.

A built-in cupboard in the corner by the window is divided, with a small door out of reach at the top. I pull up a chair, but it is locked. It is the only cupboard or drawer that is locked. I wonder what could be in it but stop short of going out to the toolshed to find something that might pry it open. It is disturbing to be in this room. A small mirror hangs above the dresser, with tools for grooming laid out in strict formation below: a hairbrush and a comb, a tray for cuff links and shirt studs, a

204 / *Charles Laurence*

worn leather manicure kit with a nail file, and tarnished scis-
sors for trimming. Nothing in this world seems to have changed
since he placed these things on the cabinet beside his old iron
cots at school and, later, in the army barracks. On the wall he
has hung prints of Constantinople and the Bosporous, his last
post abroad. They are indifferent prints, however, and you can
tell he doesn't care.

His treasures are in the corner, by the bathroom door, where
there is a small mahogany side table with a shallow drawer.
Hanging above is an oil portrait of Kate. It is a dreadful painting but perhaps not to Father, because he has hung it here. I
had forgotten all about it. But now I remember how my parents
commissioned it in Prague, after I went to boarding school, and
that there was a fuss because it was so disappointing. Kate sits
in a blue dress with a white collar, turned slightly to her right,
her eyes looking too far to the left. It is not the Kate in my
mind or in my photo album. She looks glum. The artist was
Canadian, I believe, and the fuss came when my parents asked
him to redo this part and that part. I peer closely at the pigment, and indeed I can see the reworking around Kate's face.
Her hair is too light and her body too slender for when it was
painted, and the artist has tried to give her the buds of breasts,
which she certainly did not have. The strange thing is, it looks
like a portrait of Kate painted *after* she was sick, though it was
made well before.

Below the portrait Father has stood a group of framed photographs. They are of his family, whom we hardly knew, and so
I have to work out who some of the subjects are. There is a for-
mal studio portrait of his mother, and one of his father, wearing his clergyman's dog collar, with a second of him in army

khakis. Then there are his mother's parents, the Jacksons, and a portrait of Father himself as a child with his baby brother and his sister—though, revealingly, none of the stepbrothers and -sisters his father had with a second wife. There is a photograph of Kate at seven and another of us together running toward the camera, Kate in the lead, taken that same summer when Father made us the bows and arrows. There is a miniature glass figure of the Venus de Milo and a carved Madonna and Child enclosed in a case made of olive wood from Palestine. In the center, at the back, is a candle that has not been lit. I open the drawer and take out a leather-bound Bible, and for the first time I shiver a bit as I open the cover because it is so like my own, which I have kept even though I have no faith. It was given to him, I see, when he was eight, before being sent away to school, and is inscribed: Peter H. Laurence, Easter 1930, Sialkot, Punjab, India. There are Indian coins he has kept all these years, and coins from all his travels. I carefully open an envelope and find a birthday card sent from India featuring the head of a St. Bernard, a spray of roses in yellow and red, and the printed words: "To Wish My Dear Son a Bright and Happy Birthday." A postcard from 61 Kimberly Road, Quetta, is dated 1942, when Father was on the battlefield, and begins: "My Dearest P., though I have not overwhelmed you with letters, I have had you constantly in mind wondering where you were and how you are faring." Father has stored a traveler's shaving kit in a leather case in a corner of the drawer, and below it are two small cardboard boxes. In the first is a silver pocketknife with a single blade at each end and marked with his initials, PHL. In the second I find the dress ribbon for his Military Cross, two regimental buttons, and the epaulet pips of a major. Below them are his dog tags. They are the same as the tags I was issued forty years later, when, as a journalist, I followed the Marine commandos into battle, and they are not like the ones you see in the movies. One red and one green, they are made of asbestos so that no matter how badly burned, they identify the dead, one to be left on the corpse and the second to be cut away for the records of the fallen. Father wrote me a letter on the battlefield too: "Your despatches get better and better. We are full of admiration for your hardiness in keeping up with the Commandos! Excelsior." I keep that with my own dog tags. I hold Father's tags across my palm for a long time, then slip them into my pocket and close the drawer.

Downstairs I find a bottle of Armagnac and pour myself a measure. I sit down in Father's study and stare at the top row of his bookshelves. At the center are four titles reading: *GOD*, *The Radley Register*, *Swift and Bold: The King's Royal Rifle Corps*, and *The Diplomatic List*.

"Is that you?" I hear Mother call out from upstairs.

"Yes, it's me," I answer.

"It's *terribly* late! What on earth are you doing?" I'm not quite sure how to answer this, and remain silent. "When are you going to turn the lights out?"

I get up and leave the study, glass in hand. She is on the landing, peering down over the banister. "Just pottering about," I explain. "Looking at things, sort of exploring."

Mother, coming down the first flight of stairs, looks accusingly at my drink. She is in her robe and slippers, her hair up in a net.

"Are you drunk?"

Clearly annoyed by my silence, Mother turns and takes a step back up, and then adds: "I know you're cross. You have been since my remark about Charlotte." Her voice sharpens when she is ready for a fight.

"Well, that's right," I answer. "'Course it's typical of you, isn't it? Never a lost chance to remind me of how awful my children are. So Charlotte's not worthy of your bloody jewels!"

I do not feel in the least bit drunk, and I know I am not because I am nowhere near my limit and it has been hours since dinner. But I know I am about to say things to Mother that I do not want to say, and that I want to say very much, and that I am not going to be able to stop myself from saying. My throat is tightening, and the words are growing blunter and louder in my mind.

"What would it *matter* if Charlotte sold your fucking jewels so that she could go bloody shopping in the mall? You'd be dead, wouldn't you? It has nothing to *do* with that. You just have to be nasty. You want to be mean to Charlotte. And what about Luke's sword! Remember when Father wanted to leave him his house in a generational trust, like planting his trees? How did you react to that? You'd said we'd put arsenic in your tea to get the house!"

"My God! You're jealous!" says Mother. She looks oddly triumphant.

I climb up the first flight of steps toward her: "Bull*shit*! You told me you didn't want Charlotte coming to see you because you couldn't 'deal' with her! Nothing about how you might help her."

Sensing my anger build, Mother scuttles toward her bedroom.

"And what about the time you told me you didn't love Luke?" I shout after her. "'We have no feelings for Luke.' That's what you said. He was just a fucking baby, and you had to tell me you didn't love my son!"

She turns. Now she looks puzzled. "How could we? It wasn't normal. You didn't tell us for months that Mia was pregnant. Most people know right away when a grandchild is on the way. How do you think we looked to our friends? And we hardly *knew* him."

Mother is an old lady, but suddenly she doesn't seem it. Mother is an old lady losing her husband, but all I hear is her spurning my kids. She shuts her door, but I press my face to it and shout at her. Has she ever stopped to wonder what it's like to be bent over a chair and thrashed until you bleed, even though you are just a boy and what they are doing is breaking the fucking Geneva Convention on torture? What about when Benedict was beaten for stuttering? Had she ever thought of that?

"Oh dear," she replies, muffled by the closed door. "I didn't know that—*no*, I didn't know that."

"If he told me, he'd sure as hell tell his own *mother*."

"Well, I don't remember." Her voice quiets, and I strain to hear. "I suppose it was his sports master. He was always thought of as a bit of a sadist."

I slump to the floor with my back against the door. I am starting to feel drunk, weak-kneed. I'm losing it.

"So you left him there even though the sports master was a sadist. You left him there with his stutter to be beaten by a sadist."

"Everybody goes to boarding school."

"There are two people in the world who are responsible for Benedict being beaten by a sadist, Mother. Father, and *you*."

I stand up now and open Mother's bedroom door.

"Have you gone mad? I'll call for help!"

Mother has family photographs on every surface, and figurines of cats—not cluttered but gracefully laid out. She has got back into bed and parked her slippers on the rug. The heavy curtains are drawn tight as she cannot sleep with either sound or moonlight. The bedside lamp is on. "I want to talk about Kate."

"Oh, God."

"What happened to Kate?"

"Why do you go *on* about it?"

"I want to know what happened. You know I've been to Prague, and you know what I've been doing there, so don't lie."

Mother moves to the far side of the bed, turns away, and pulls the covers over her head. I don't think I am shouting.

"Did Mucha fuck Kate? Did Kate see Mucha fucking *you*? Did someone else fuck Kate?"

"There was that Milos boy," Mother says from under the covers. "We always wondered if he might have done something."

"I don't believe it. That's an excuse. What about that arsehole French teacher?"

"I don't think so, but I don't know. I don't know if anything happened."

"Mucha would fuck anyone, that's one thing I've found out. He had teenage girls around his house. Did you know *that*?"

She is silent now. "Why did you take her to his house, to that cottage of his?"

"I know George was a most immoral man, but I don't *think* he did anything with Kate."

"Well, she must have known pretty bloody well what you were doing in the cottage. And how did *that* make her feel about Dad?"

"She would never have seen anything!"

"Don't lie. I remember the place. I've got a fucking photograph of it that I took when I came up there with Dad. Remember? Jesus, Mother—there's nowhere private in a place like that. John slept in that cubicle in the kitchen."

"No, no, no! It was never inside! Geraldine and George slept upstairs, and Kate and I would be downstairs." Mother's head is up on the pillow now. She is looking away, toward the window.

"I told you I've read the files. Geraldine's being there would make no difference to Mucha. He'd fuck you anyway. There is *no* way Kate would not have known."

"We went *outside*. Into the field, in the woods. *There!*"

I do not know how long it is that I stand there, that she lies there, saying nothing. I sit on the edge of the bed. The light is dim, and it's hard to see my mother's face.

"How many others?" I finally ask. "Jiří. Flash . . . Harry in Berlin? There's a Berlin lover in the files too."

"There were others. It's true. But I'm not about to tell you!"

"How does that make you feel about Dad? You always said he was the love of your life. Just a few hours ago I heard him tell you he loves you."

"Oh dear! Oh dear! I know I don't really deserve it. He is *Peter*, my rock. Peter actually means rock, did you know that? He is head and shoulders above the others."

Mother is crying now, gently, without fuss. "Does he mean it, do you think? Can he really mean it, that he loves me?"

Father's dog tags are in my pocket, and I touch them with my fingers. "I think I should leave now," I say after a moment. "Yes," says Mother, holding a tissue. I hesitate a moment. "Go!" she snaps. "*Get out!*"

Sixteen

Geraldine peers from her window overlooking Castle Square, just as she did when I visited her before, and takes a few minutes to get down to the heavy front door. "How lovely to see you again," she says brightly. This time I have brought Scottish shortbread, and flowers too. We make our way through the stone vaulting and old treasures to the stairs and on up to the grand hall that is the living room. I stop in front of Alphonse Mucha's life-size poster of Sarah Bernhardt as Medea. It has faded in the hundred years or so since it was made, the colors brought back only in the new prints and minia- ture versions on offer in the Mucha museum's souvenir shop.

"You know, I went back there and bought a couple after I came to see you and noticed it," I say. The upturned face of Medea's dead son sprawled below her dagger is as lovely as any Alphonse ever drew. But Bernhardt's eyes are not narrowed with the traditional fury of her revenge; rather they are huge with horror and surprise. "Odd that, isn't it?" I say to Geral- dine. She has come to stand by my shoulder, gazing at Medea, familiar after all these years. "Alphonse hasn't made her evil. Maybe he couldn't do evil."

Geraldine laughs her little laugh. "There's a story to that, you know," she says. "When they wanted Bernhardt to do Medea, she read the play and loved the drama but didn't want to ruin her image by playing someone so horrid. So they changed it for her! They changed it so as to make it seem Medea had been provoked beyond endurance by her sons. So in that way it wasn't her fault that she killed them, and she could look surprised by what she did! Jiří always said that when Bernhardt came to the studio to pose, she demanded that Alphonse paint her just like that. She was very demanding, you know. Now, let's have tea."

We settle before the same fireplace with the black marble devil thrusting out in bas relief, and Geraldine lights the gas ring under the kettle before sitting back to wait for it to boil. "I heard that your father died. I'm so sorry, Charles. John sent the obituary from the *Telegraph*. Just lovely. Did you write it? No? Well, it was beautifully done, I thought." It seems extraordinary, I say to Geraldine, that when I saw her just a year ago he had still been a man in full life. The end had been fast, and that was perhaps a mercy.

It had been the same with Jiří, she says: a mercy. "I have had a few problems myself, which is most unlike me! I fell on the steps of the concert hall in the winter, and of course because I am such an old lady everyone thought I had broken a hip. I hadn't! Not me! But I did tear the skin on my shin, and when I was in the hospital they found a little cancer. They gave me radiation treatment for seven weeks to burn out a tumor behind my ear. So I'm well again! But I am very tired." I tell

Geraldine that she has a terrific constitution and that maybe she will go on forever. She laughs and fills the teapot with boiling water. There are scones and butter, and Geraldine urges me to eat up.

Outside the light is beginning to dim beyond the Hrad and the Cathedral spire. It has been a blue-sky day. "We've had almost no snow this year," she says, "almost none at all. I think it's this global warming going on." Today Geraldine is wearing a blue shirt buttoned to the neck, which sets off the cool of her pale blue eyes. The eye that wept on my first visit has healed, it seems, and is now dry and healthy. She draws a heavy cardigan knitted in bright patterns close around her when she sits. Geraldine must have performed this ritual of wary hospitality time and time again, I think, wondering how I am going to broach the subject of spies and sex and betrayal.

"The police came to see me once," she begins, after I do direct the conversation that way. "Here, in this house. I saw them in the kitchen downstairs, and a cat was having kittens. Literally, in her basket, while I talked to the secret policemen. Really, I was more interested in the cat having kittens than in talking to them.

"ANTY? No, I don't think I did know that Jiří had been named that by the police. No, I don't think I did. But you see, when you came out of jail in those days, you simply had to cooperate, and Jiří had no option. Nor did anyone else. It was part of life. Jiří knew everyone. Diplomats, foreign dignitaries . . . they all came to see him, and he enjoyed that. So of course the authorities wanted him to be involved. But I'll describe what he did for them by telling you what he told me: it was like that novel by Graham Greene, *Our Man in Havana*, with the character who made up stories to give to British intelligence, which he was working for. He told them things so that he could stay in Havana, because if you remember he did not want to leave Havana. That's how it was for Jiří. He wanted to live in Prague. And that's why the authorities got fed up and sacked him, because in the end he told them nothing."

I butter a scone, though I am not actually hungry. The dusk through the window has turned late-winter bleak.

"Yes, I do remember Kamil Pixa—I remember him from the days when Jiří worked at Barrandov, on the film scripts. They were *desperate* for film scripts. I didn't like him, though. But he was involved with Jiří *before* Jiří went to jail? I don't remember that. Perhaps I didn't know. I didn't know Pixa was important in the ministry. It was hard to tell. As for Ian Milner, a KGB spy? Really! We knew he was an old Communist, but he was such a shy, retiring sort of man.

"I suppose they all had to report back on what was going on in their lives. I did think that Jiří reported back on his diplomatic contacts, yes, because that is what they would have been so interested in. Do I think that Jiří was working for British Intelligence too? Well, that's a thought! And you know he did know everyone, and he had been a pilot in the war. It could be!"

Geraldine watches me drain the old china teacup and sees a chance to break the conversation for the moment. She is calm but a little uncomfortable too. There is so much in the past to talk about and so much that is better left unsaid. She staggers for a moment on the narrow hearth rug, the devil at her back, as she stoops to pour more tea. She fumbles the tea strainer and it clatters against its saucer. I lean forward to help her.

"Of course I knew about your mother and what was going on, but, as I already said, I did not interfere with Jiří's private life. He took her and Kate to Jiřetín, I remember that. A few times. I remember your mother was a very elegant person. She *did* cause trouble, though—for Jiří and for everyone else.

"Women were very attracted to Jiří. And he liked women. My attitude, though, was that, after all that had happened to him, no one had a right to interfere in his private life. He had to live, to be alive, to live as he wanted to. The orgies and so on—that was exaggerated. Jiří let people come over to our house because no one had any privacy left—living, you know, in their little flats that the authorities had divided up. They could come here and get away from those lives. Of course some people took advantage. And many of his contacts—his lovers, his orgy friends—didn't even know I existed. I was with John. I had John to look after."

Geraldine's laugh for once has a bitter edge, and she knows that I catch it. She rests again, hunched in a way that is new to her. I hope that she is not stopping now. But I needn't worry.

"People thought: 'There's something wrong with her, to put up with it. She doesn't care! She has no feelings!' Then, in the 1970s when I went back to Scotland, they said: 'There! She's left him!' But I only did that so he could get his exit visa and get abroad, because at the time that was the rule: a man could go abroad to visit his family if he was divorced. When the authorities clamped down again, after the Prague Spring, it was harder for Jiří to get the visa to promote his father's art. But Jiří never split from me, and I never left Jiří. He was my husband, and when I could, I came back to Prague to be with

him." Geraldine has been loyal. In her own way, she has always
been loyal.

This time the silence stretches on. Geraldine looks at me,
then looks away. She switches on a light, and when the telephone rings she gets up with her hands pushing against the
arms of her chair. She makes the few steps to her desk, takes
the handset from a pile of papers, and answers. It is a friend
talking about a planned outing to yet another concert. Perhaps
it is the piano that has sustained her all these years; always another note to hear. She tells the friend that she must go because
she has a guest for tea. I help her shuffle the dishes into order
on the tray, but we leave them there on the table in front of the
fire. I get up now, thinking it might be time to leave Geraldine
alone. But she gestures for me to sit down. "When we held
Jiří's funeral," she says, "we wanted a writer—any one of his
colleagues—to read from one of his books. No one would do it.
They said they didn't really know him. No one knew who Jiří
really was. Who he worked for. Which side he was on. Yes, he
was shadowy. But then he lived in a shadowy world."

We are finished now. Geraldine picks up her keys for the
dead-bolt locks that secure her way though the worn old palace
to the safety of her bed, with her piano close at its side. She
is free to come and go, and this is her world now. On the way
back though the Mucha rooms, I tell her that Father suggested
that I should ask her about the two-way mirror fitted for the
photographers, and so I will.

This time I get a real Geraldine laugh, head back, throat
up. "Oh, no! There's no two-way mirror! *But* . . . look how
these mirrors are arranged: photographers would look into one

mirror to take pictures at the other end of the room! I've seen them do that."

Geraldine turns the lock behind me and is gone. A memory of Kate skips smiling over the pavement as wide as a carriage drive. She is in her lycée uniform and racing to ring the bell, a vision gone just as quickly as it came. Strange what you remember, and now these memories dart out unexpectedly, blurred by speed.

Every good spy story needs a killing at its end, some freelance assassination in the name of justice. But I have never killed anyone and cannot even imagine the feel of it, and suddenly there seems to be no one left to kill. Jiří Mucha is dead. And his need to live, to be alive, has long since sucked dry the lives of so many others. I understand that I wanted Geraldine to tell me what he had done to Kate, to stoke my rage to exhaustion with pornographic visions of little girls trying so hard to please and screaming at tight entry, whatever the skill or poisoned charm. But she has not, and maybe there *is* no such thing to tell. I know at last that it makes no difference.

It makes no difference because what happened is that Kate was taken to a place of cruelty and betrayal which was its own violation. She is another story in the shadows of Prague. Mucha was a shadowy man because he lived in a shadowy world. He had it in him to do whatever it took to survive, and he did it. But he is dead now, dead because at the end no one will read at his funeral. No one knew who he was, and his story is forever denied its echo through the transepts of memories held in love.

The night is quiet. I will walk back to the Nové Město and drink absinthe at the Café Ripka, where old Soviet typewriters are mounted on the wall as trophies because words are defiance when they are true. I walk through the gardens of the square under the light of the single lamppost as big as a tree, almost monstrous, and on to the black iron statue commemorating medieval plagues, saints wailing with faces as hard as their faith. The guard changes at the gates of the Hrad, jackboots slapping the cobbles. Herculean statues perched above the gates cudgel and sword would-be intruders in acts of gross violence. I hurry down the steep-stepped street toward the baroque cathedral of the Hapsburgs at the heart of *Malá* Strana, a fat bourgeoise at her chocolate cake and coffee. I pass the bust of Churchill keeping watch outside the British embassy, where a light is glowing in the guardroom. Churchill, who watched Czechoslovakia be traded to the Communists just as it had been to the Nazis; who abandoned Prague to sex without joy when there *was* no other freedom.

The Ripka is busy and filled with smoke. There is laughter among the young who dream of being poets and writers and perhaps even authors of great liberations. I find a seat at the back against the library shelves, below the showily mounted typewriters. A waiter snakes through the din with jugs of beer and trays of shotglasses, and takes my order for absinthe which will come pale green with a jug of water on the side. A homeless man comes in dragging bags and bumping chairs, and no one stops him. He takes a spare seat, without asking, at a table of men with shallow beards and a woman with a scarf thrown around her neck. But they are talking, each in turn, with their faces almost touching, their eyes shining, and say nothing to the man whose stink rises even above the cigarette smoke. Finally seeming to notice him, they just buy him beer, after which he shuffles off to the bathrooms. I sip my drink and stare at the books without needing to try to translate their titles, because I know my own story now.

In the morning I meet Tom, and he fetches his car from the basement garage of the glass and brass Novotel, which is in a different world. We slip through the traffic, our big German tires thumping on the tram tracks as we cross them, looking for Expressway 65 which will take us northeast into the mountains and Poland. I am going to find the *chata* at Jiřetín because I want to see it again, just once. Geraldine has done her best to tell me where it is. Jiřetín pod Bukovou, in the Jizerské Mountains. "John has been doing it up a bit," she has said. "You'll see the improvements. I'm afraid it's rather difficult to find. John has got to know some of the locals, so your best bet will be to ask for the Mucha cottage." I have the old photograph in my pocket and a memory of its setting, on a green among other cottages. Tom sets the route and destination into the car's navigation system, but its commands serve only to get us lost, as this is not a journey you can track with computers from outer space.

We pass the landscape of collective farms and towns with church domes ringed by concrete intersections, and beyond them climb to a dairy country of patched-up medieval barns standing deep in mud. It is farther than I thought. The roads narrow, and Tom swoops around turns through banks of pine. From time to time there is an abandoned mill straddling the stream below, its windows long since broken but its boast of weaving fine cloth still clear in the brickwork.

At Tanvald we draw into the town square and look for coffee. There is no café on the square, but we find a store where the shopkeeper can speak enough English to sell us a local map and point the way to Jiřetín. We follow roads drawn in white along the gulley of the Kamenicė River, where some of the cloth mills are still in operation. There is ice in the shallows and snow still beneath the trees.

Now at Jiřetín there is a café, and we stop for two cups each and pastries because we have been on the road for a long time. The girl in the café is Polish, married to a Czech, but they are going to close up and move to Poland because there is no business here. She puts a log in the stove. She calls her husband, who spreads out our map and shows us where the lane turns across the river to Jiřetín pod Bukovou. There *are* old *chatas* there, and they will be on the right if we keep going for two or three miles. The bridge runs between two mills; I have no memory of such a scene and so wonder if we have come all this way to the wrong place.

The road climbs to a village that is nothing like the village in my mind. A man is hauling bags from the trunk of his car, and when I ask, "*Chata* Mucha?" he pauses to make out the words, then smiles and waves us on and gestures to the right. We pass the sign marking the end of the village, and beyond it the valley is empty. Tom pulls over, and we think we should turn around and search again. But the flank of a meadow rising to the right looks slightly familiar, and I urge him on. Quite suddenly we see it—the *chata*, beyond the sloping green, exactly where it should be. I can see the water well. I hold the photograph against the car window, and it is a match with three windows to the left of a closed-in porch around the front door, with two to the right. There is snow on the bank. Just as Geraldine promised, Mucha's *chata* has a new red roof.

The track soon turns to ice, and Tom pulls up. I step out to scramble up the last few yards. At the top of the bank I stand up straight, and now I can touch the past. There is the spot where Kate stood with John against the hewn log wall, and where I must have shaken the camera as I pressed the shutter button, as that particular snapshot is blurred. Still, you can see that Kate has had a bad haircut with a pudding-bowl fringe. And you can see, too, that both are smiling, not posing, simply happy. Their arms are touching, but they are not holding hands; they are just children.

A fir tree has grown tall in front of the *chata* where there was none. I go a few paces along the path and turn with my back to the sun and see where Mucha had stood with his arms around Mother and Kate, Father and Geraldine standing just behind them. Mucha's big Chrysler is gone, of course. I slide down to the well and pull open the door to the well house. No trout is trapped there now. Instead a pump has been dug into the ground in front of the well with a pipeline running straight up to the building.

The doors are locked. Light glaring off the snow is making it hard to see in through the windows, and some are obscured by blinds. I cup my hands to my eyes and see a hard-worn table and some wooden chairs and upholstered chairs pushed together in a corner, partly covered with a sheet, because the *chata* is closed. From the back I see a second floor built out at right angles with a back door and a loft in the eaves above. Mother was right about the upstairs, and peering through another window I can make out a narrow open stairway between the kitchen range and the space that made the downstairs bedroom. In my mind I hear voices laughing around the kitchen table.

Tom comes up, and we poke around together looking for clues and working cameras. I explain my memories as best I can. A few minutes later Tom says he is going back to the car but needs to take a pee before we leave. He looks around for a private spot because there are the other homes scattered around the green, a few parked cars even, and maybe a few curious eyes as well. I tell him that I am glad we both had two cups of coffee, because I am planning to piss right here on George's cottage. Tom snorts and unzips and splashes onto the snow. "Fucking Commie spy!" he shouts out. I walk around to the back again and wonder whether if I aim right I can piss under the back door. Hitting the step itself at first, I adjust, crouching down a bit to get the right angle, and that way I get some in under the threshold. I refuse to feel ashamed, and I keep on until I am dry.

After that I go to the front and stand still by the porch. The landscape of hills and low mountains with snow in steep valleys, and Alpine trees, stretches far further than it had in my mind's eye. Rough cut from the centuries, it endures.

Back on that summer Sunday in 1959, the cars are parked on the grass, and when it's time to go, in the late afternoon, we spill out from around the table. Now everyone, including Nanny with my little brother, gathers for the photograph, if only to please me, before saying their goodbyes. Mother says we can swap rides, and I can go home with her in her little white Fiat. Kate can be with Father, and she will like that, as she has not seen him all weekend.

I climb in as Mother kisses Jiří Mucha on the cheek, kicking out a leg as she slips behind the wheel. She changes to sunglasses, for we will be driving toward the sun. The punk-punk rattle and roar of the engine chimes in to the rear as she dips the clutch and crunches into gear, and we are off over the track, bouncing with our hands up, waving.

I follow the road with my eye through the valley and into the hills as in memory we speed through sunshine spilling shadows of pines over the road to create the dizzying effect of a strobe. I shut my eyes now, straining to bring back the picture of my mother in something white, her pale arms free of sleeves for once, as the sun weakens, a scarf tied over her head against the wind because the roof is rolled back. The engine roars and clatters on behind us. It feels terrifically fast, though we can't be doing more than fifty miles an hour or so, zinging down through the gears for the bends, Mother laughing and pressing a low-heeled shoe to the floor. She looks at me, smiling, and shouts out: "The engine's really a motorbike engine, you know! And because it's behind us, it sounds like we're being chased but never caught!" She urges her little white car down the straight, and there is joy in her face when she laughs like that. How many times has Mucha seen that face?

My heart beats a little faster, as it always did with the speed and exhilaration, and then I hear the sound of a second engine behind us, a cacophony of two. I twist around until I am on my knees, facing out over the furled roof to watch a tractor-red Jawa motorcycle, Czechoslovakia's best, coursing ever closer with plumes of smoke trailing and a lean of pure excitement as it tips into corners, and behind the handlebars a head with hair streaming and eyes shrouded by goggles. I see the rider's face stretching against his own private gale.

"A race!" Mother cries out. "A race!" And she dashes ahead with both hands on the steering wheel, holding the road and staying in front, and we are laughing together because it is so much fun, and there is triumph each time the man on the motorbike comes close, only to fall behind again. Not even two engines behind can catch us! And nothing can catch Mother and me that night as we race all the way back to the rattling cobblestones of Prague.

Opening my eyes again, I am still in front of the *chata*, and there is a longing that is not quite love but alive and coursing within, and for that, at least, there may be hope in a time of rotten endings.

Index

A NOTE ON THE AUTHOR

Born in London and educated in England, Charles
Laurence is a former foreign correspondent for the
London *Telegraph* who covered conflicts ranging
from the Falklands War to the Middle East, India,
and Afghanistan before heading the paper's New York
bureau. Now an American citizen, he continues to
write for British newspapers and magazines and lives
in Woodstock, New York, and the Caribbean island
of Salt Cay.

ACKNOWLEDGMENTS

For their encouragement,
and their editorial guidance, special thanks to
Richard L. Archer, Cynthia Maude-Gembler,
David List and Gerald R. Gioglio.